STUDY GUIDE

Janice Brandon-Falcone
Northwest Missourie State University

Sixth Edition

Volume I: to 1877

THESE
UNITED STATES
The Questions of Our Past

Irwin Unger
New York University

PRENTICE HALL
Englewood Cliffs, New Jersey 07632

©1995 by PRENTICE-HALL, INC.
A Simon and Schuster Company
Englewood Cliffs, New Jersey 07632

10 9 8 7 6 5 4 3 2

ISBN 0-13-171505-4
Printed in the United States of America

Contents

Preface

This Study Guide is designed to accompany

THESE UNITED STATES by Irwin Unger

Sixth Edition, Volume I

This Guide contains the following items for each chapter:

1.   Summary and Outline

2.   Learning Objectives

3.   Identifications

4.   Focus Your Reading

5.   Questions: Multiple Choice and Essay

6.   Map Excersises in Selected Chapters

The New World Encounters the Old

Why 1492?

Summary and Outline

Summary: Two groups "discovered" the New World before Columbus: the American Indians and the Scandinavian Norsemen. What then is the significance of the year 1492?

Outline: **I. The First Americans:**   The first settlers of the New World were Asian migrants from Siberia who settled in both North and South America, numbering about 75 million by 1492. They developed distinct languages, agriculture and diverse social and political structures comparable to Asia and Europe.

A.   The North American Setting

A temperate climate, a central basin of limited rainfall, and abundant natural resources marked the North American continent.

B.   The Great Indian Civilizations

The most advanced American people were the Maya, who had a written language, mathematics and knowledge of astronomy. To the north in Mexico, Aztecs formed a centralized empire based on military conquest; an even larger empire was organized in South America by the Incas of Peru, who built sturdy fortresses in the Andes mountains.

C.   The Indians of North America

About nine million Indians lived in what is now the United States. Some were peaceful like the Iroquois; others were warlike like the Delaware. Almost all had religious beliefs which were based on the forces of nature. They did not regard land as private property but as cooperative tribal possession. This concept was to cause problems when the Europeans arrived.

II.   The First European "Discovery":

The first Europeans to see the Labrador coast were sailors led by a Norwegian named Bjarni Herjulfsson, who was blown off course in 986 on a voyage to Greenland. In 1000, Leif Ericsson wintered in Vinland and an attempt was made to colonize what was later Newfoundland, but the settlement did not last, and other Europeans forgot about the Norse discoveries.

III.   The Rise of Modern Europe:

Medieval Europe: Europeans were unable to follow up on Norse settlements because they were a weak and divided people until the twelfth century. Trade and commerce were not congenial to the Christian society of the Middle Ages; the great monarchies which were to dominate the modern period were not yet strong enough to organize the resources needed for extensive colonial enterprises.

IV. European Revival:

A. The Lure of the East

Western European Christians were content with a rather low level of economy and culture until they encountered sophisticated Muslim civilization during the eleventh-century Crusades. By the fourteenth century, European merchants had also discovered the products of the Far East. Spices for food, flavor and preservation and money changing were embraced eagerly by medieval Europeans. Cash brought a breakdown of the feudal system and the end of serfdom. Cities were reborn and prosperity based on trade and banking came to be the basis of a new way of life.

B. The Nation State

The new urban classes of Europe wanted peace and order. The most effective way to get them was to support the monarchs who could impose national taxes. The new nation states could mobilize resources on a much larger scale than earlier religious and feudal states. They could organize exploration and conquest of previously unknown peoples thousands of miles away.

C. Revolutions in Thought and Communication

New contacts with classical antiquity enriched European culture and produced a new secular attitude called "humanism." The invention of printing encouraged literacy and created a communications revolution that highlighted the scientific nature of the American discovery in 1492.

D. New Technology

Advances in navigation made European maritime knowledge more exact in 1492 than in the year 1000. The compass, quadrant, and astrolabe were accompanied by improvements in ship design. More maneuverable and stable vessels made it possible to undertake long ocean voyages. Gunpowder allowed Europeans to undertake the full-scale conquest of the Native American populations.

V. European Expansion:

The European quest to find other lands was started by Prince Henry the Navigator of Portugal, who sponsored voyages to Africa and the Atlantic islands. The Portuguese explorer Da Gama reached India by 1449; by 1550 the Portuguese controlled the East Indian spice trade.

A. Columbus and the Spanish Exploration

Columbus' scheme to help Spain counter the Portuguese was to sail west to reach the Far East. Under the sponsorship of Queen Isabella, Columbus took ten weeks to cross the

Atlantic Ocean. He followed his first voyage to the Caribbean with three others, thereby establishing the first permanent European communities in the New World. Spain also sent Magellan around the world in 1519, proving finally that the Americas were two continents previously unknown to the Europeans.

B.   Spain Encounters the Indian Civilizations

In 1519 Hernando Cortes landed in Mexico and conquered the Aztec capital of Tenochtitlan. He was aided by the ruling class's belief that white gods would arrive to rule the Aztecs. Francisco Pizarro accomplished a similar feat in Peru in 1532, strangling the Inca emperor, Atahualpa after receiving a roomful of gold. In both instances guns and horses made it possible for a few Spaniards to conquer large Native American empires. By 1550, the Maya had fallen to the Europeans as well.

C.   Spain's Rivals

Precious metals and new products from America made Spain the richest and most powerful nation in sixteenth-century Europe. England and France joined the scramble for wealth and colonies after the discoveries of John Cabot and Giovanni da Verrazano. The Dutch hired Henry Hudson to find a water route through North America. At the same time several French explorers were moving into the heartland of North America.

VI.   **The Columbian Exchange:**

Europe Benefits: Europeans removed Indian self-rule thoroughly and quickly. The life of Indians in Spanish America resembled that of European serfs. They were better off in English America only because they were fewer in number and could escape their captors. Indians died off rather quickly from European diseases, especially smallpox. Massive assaults on their economic systems and religious and cultural life left the survivors impoverished. On the other hand, Europeans benefited from the contact with America, not only in terms of wealth, but also an expanded diet. Botanical discoveries enriched European science; and contact with new peoples encouraged the origins of anthropology and sociology.

VII. **Conclusions:**

1492 was a turning point in the history of the world. The inhabitants of the New World suffered while their Old World conquerors prospered, and indeed prepared to send more of their number across the Atlantic.

Learning Objectives

After reading Chapter 1 you should be able to:

1.   Describe the cultures of the North and South American Indians before discovery.

2.   Identify the earliest Europeans to settle in the New World.

3.   Explain the developments in European history that favored voyages of exploration and conquest in the New World.

4.   Account for the significance of the year 1492.

5.   Describe the Spanish conquest of the major Native American civilizations.

6.   Discuss the Columbian exchange for both the Europeans and the Indians.

Identifications

Identify the following terms as you read the chapter; also note the significance of the term.

1.   maize   2.   Mayas

3.   Aztecs   4.   Incas

5.   Iroquois Confederacy,   6.   pantheists
      or Six Nations

7.   Middle Ages   8.   vassals

9.   spice islands   10.   burghers

11.   Prince Henry, the   12.   Christopher Columbus
      Navigator

13.   Hernando Cortes   14.   Francisco Pizarro

Focus Your Reading

Employ the terms you have identified above in answering the following questions:

1.   What economic and political changes in Europe motivated exploration and travel in the 15th and 16th centuries?

2.   Discuss the culture, politics and economy of several of the Indian groups which Europeans met.

3.   Discuss the Columbian exchange on both sides in terms of animals, food, disease and technology.

4.   List the animals now present in the New World that came from the Old World. Which of these are useful for purposes other than eating? Compare this with a list of food products that traveled from the New World to the Old World. Which of these products are now staples in the European and American diet?

5.   Why were the great Indian leaders Moctezuma ll of Mexico and Atahualpa of Peru so easily subdued by the small force of Spanish conquistadors that invaded them?

Upon what attitudes did the Europeans base their confidence that they could accomplish these tasks.

Questions

Multiple Choice

1. Which two groups stumbled on the Americas before Columbus?
   a. Indians and Norse
   b. Norse and Italian
   c. Irish and Norse explorers
   d. Spaniards and Portuguese

2. The Mayans had calculated all the following except:
   a. the idea of zero
   b. the earth as the center of the universe
   c. the cycles of the seasons
   d. the times of the eclipses

3. The Native Americans differed from Europeans in their attitudes concerning:
   a. individual possession of land and natural resources
   b. the use of the land
   c. the accumulation of wealth
   d. all of the above

4. Following the fall of the Roman Empire most Europeans lived as :
   a. slaves
   b. unfree peasants or serfs
   c. vassals
   d. free-farmers

5. The institution that held Europe together during the Middle Ages was:
   a. the Holy Roman Empire
   b. the small merchant class
   c. the Roman Catholic Church
   d. the Protestant Church

6. Crucial to the growth of capitalism and the decline of feudalism was:
   a. the revival of trade and commerce
   b. the just price policy of the church
   c. the otherworldly, largely illiterate population of 1000 A.D.
   d. the largely literate clergy

7. Which of the following did not prepare Europeans for overseas ventures?
   a. the invention of movable type
   b. the self-sufficient manorial economy
   c. advances in naval architecture
   d. simple navigational instruments

8. Columbus established permanent settlements in all of the following except:

a. Hispaniola
b. Puerto Rico
c. Mexico
d. Cuba

9. Which of the following factors defeated the Aztecs between 1519 and 1521?
   a. the myth of the white gods
   b. horses and firearms
   c. Indian trust and fear
   d. all of the above

10. The difference between the Spanish conquest of Peru and Mexico was that in the instance of the Incas:
    a. the Spanish forces could achieve no quick victory
    b. Atahualpa escaped capture to lead guerrilla movements
    c. Pizarro used honest tactics to defeat the Indians
    d. all of the above

11. Sponsored by Henry VII of England, the explorer John Cabot was able to establish English claims at:
    a. the Carolina coast
    b. Nova Scotia and Chesapeake Bay
    c. New York
    d. all of the above

12. The Europeans probably brought all of the following diseases to America except:
    a. tuberculosis
    b. smallpox
    c. syphilis
    d. measles

Essay

1. Discuss the Indian settlement of the American continents. Where did they come from, where did they go, and what connections did they have with the Old World?

2. Discuss Columbus' own account of his voyage. What unique events would you not know about unless you read his original account?

3. What was the long-term impact of European settlement in the New World? What portions of Native American civilization were changed? Which changes were for the better and which for the worse? Explain why you think so in each case.

4. Discuss the life and reign of Isabella of Castille. What did she feel compelled to do to assert her authority over the aristocrats? What was done to ferret out non-Catholics? How did Columbus benefit from changes overseen by Isabella?

Map Exercises

Locate or draw in on the following two maps the locations listed below and explain their significance.

1. Atlantic Ocean

2. Gold Coast and Slave Coast of Africa

3. South America

4. Isthmus of Panama

5. Territory claimed by Spain

6. Territory claimed by Portugal

7. Aztec Empire

8. Inca Empire

9. Spain

10. Portugal

11. Hispaniola

12. San Salvador

13. West Africa

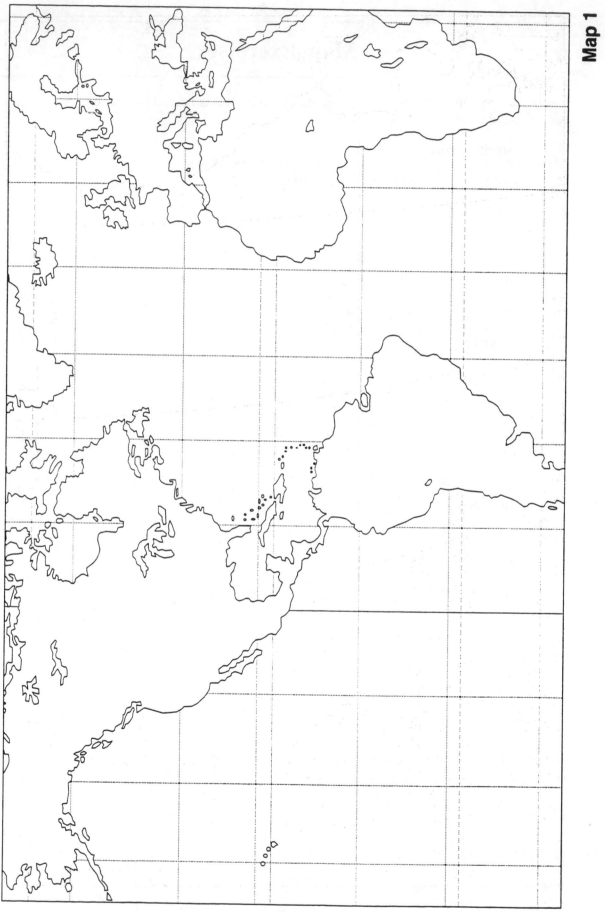

Map 1

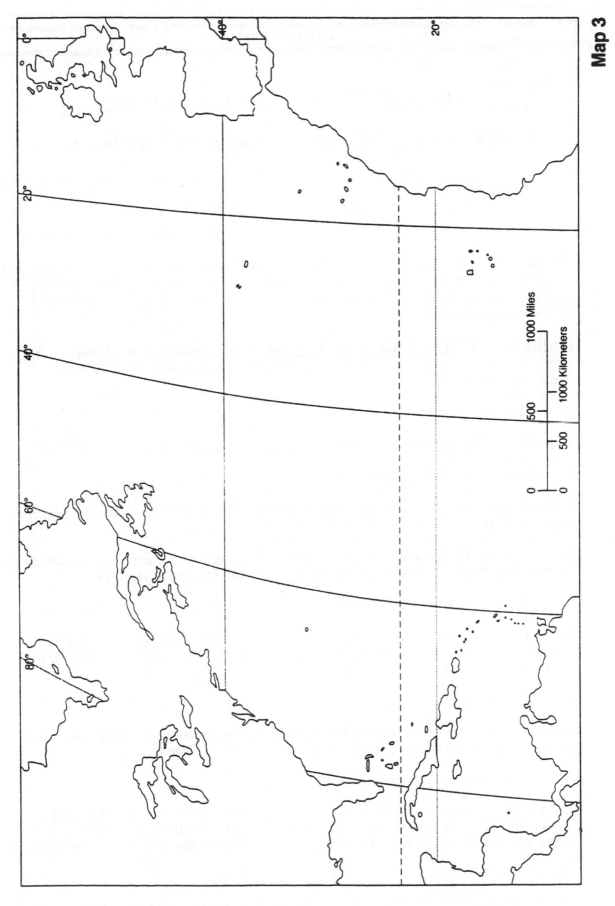

Map 3

9

CHAPTER 2

The Old World Comes to America

What brought Europeans and Africans to the New World?

Summary and Outline

Summary: Despite many risks, fears and discomforts settlers staked their lives and promoters gambled their money on America in the seventeenth century. Why did they come: was it wealth, adventure, social prestige; or were they looking for religious and political independence?

Outline: I. <u>**The Aristocratic Impulse:**</u> The second and third sons of the English aristocracy came to America to enjoy the life of gentlemen. Some of them reluctantly became businessmen.

A.   The Roanoke Attempts

Sir Walter Raleigh's plan to place colonists in Virginia failed between 1585 and 1587.

B.   Aristocratic Entrepreneurs:

Several nobles attempted to set up "proprietary" feudal estates in Maryland, the Carolinas, and New York.

II.   <u>The Profit Motive:</u>   Noble schemes for colonies were not as successful as the schemes of private promoters who wanted to gain profit from such ventures.

A.   Mercantilism and the Nation State

Mercantilism was a foreign policy that used war to gain gold and silver. Lacking these resources, England conceived of an alternate system that used colonies to supply both commodities and markets for English goods.

B.   Merchants and Profits

Commercial investors raised capital for colonial ventures by selling shares in joint-stock trading companies in which all shared either their success or failure.

C.   Jamestown: A Commercial Enterprise

Under the leadership of John Smith and Sir Thomas Dale, Jamestown was founded in Virginia in 1607. The colony survived starvation and Indian attacks to become the first permanent English settlement in Colonial America. At first the sponsor of Jamestown, the

London Company, prospered with the sale of tobacco and established the first representative colonial assembly, the House of Burgesses. However, like other joint-stock companies in the English colonies, the company ultimately failed. Virginia became a royal colony in 1624.

III. **"The Best Poor Man's Country":** The bulk of the immigrants to America were drawn from the ranks of English common people -- farmers, craftsmen and workers -- both men and women.

A. Mixed Motives

The impression that many who came to the New World were criminals fleeing the law is contradicted by the evidence that shows that most immigrants were farmers and craftsmen who were escaping from low wages, high rents and the European economic depression.

B. High Wages and Cheap Land

Colonial promoters exaggerated the attractions of the New World; however, hard work and enterprise paid off for many who utilized the untapped resources of the new continent.

C. Indentured Servants

Unskilled laborers were willing to exchange seven years of hard work for passage to America; while their lives were difficult, many eventually established themselves as independent farmers or craftsmen.

IV. **Involuntary Immigrants:** Some laborers came to English America against their will because large landowners needed cheap labor to exploit commercial crops.

A. Involuntary European Immigrants

In addition to the many young and naive immigrants who were sold into indentured service, many convicts were sent to the colonies, especially the plantations of Virginia and Maryland.

B. African Slaves

Labor-short plantation owners resorted to the purchase of "heathen" African slaves, arguing that they would benefit from Christian civilization. By law these slaves could be bought, sold, or inherited.

V. **America as a Religious Haven:** Europeans from all levels of society came to the English colonies to find religious freedom.

A. The Reformation

As a response to the worldliness of the Roman Catholic clergy, Martin Luther started the Protestant reform movement in Germany, which emphasized the equality of all Christians before God. An Anglican Church was set up in England shortly thereafter ; and the Calvinist sect within it, eventually called "Puritans," insisted that faith came to individuals by God's grace. Later Baptists and Quakers would claim that conscience was the source of moral values.

B.   The Pilgrims of Plymouth

A small group of Puritan separatists settled at Cape Cod Bay in 1620 after signing the Mayflower Compact, which established a government at Plymouth with the power to enact "just and equal laws."

C.   The Massachusetts Bay Puritans

Under the leadership of John Winthrop, prominent English Puritans secured a royal charter and founded the Massachusetts Bay Colony in 1630.

D.   Offshoots of the Massachusetts Bay Colony

Winthrop and other Puritan leaders in Massachusetts did not welcome unorthodox. When he disagreed with their views that church membership should be required for voting, Thomas Hooker was banished to Connecticut. Roger Williams left the colony because he criticized the Puritan view of taxation; he settled in Providence, Rhode Island, with others who agreed that state and church should be separated. Anne Hutchinson was declared a heretic when she challenged the notion of female subordination.

E.   Penn's Woods

A land grant by Charles II to William Penn, a wealthy Quaker, in 1681, resulted in the settlement of the tolerant colony of Pennsylvania, where the legislature imposed no taxes without consent and all religions were tolerated.

F.   The Limits of Religious Toleration

Toleration was the exception rather than the rule in the seventeenth century; many colonies restricted worship and collected tithes, taxes imposed on all citizens to support established churches.

VI.   Conclusions: Economic opportunity was the most powerful motive for the migration of ordinary English people to the New World. While many others came to worship as they chose, many more were transported to Colonial America in some system of involuntary servitude.

Learning Objectives

After reading Chapter 2, you should be able to:

1.   Explain the main reasons that Europeans both promoted and participated in colonizations of North America.

2.   Recognize the names of the principal organizers and leaders of the earliest settlements in Virginia, Maryland, New York, New Jersey, Delaware, Pennsylvania, South Carolina, Georgia and the colonies of New England.

3.   Analyze the motives of commercial entrepreneurs as well as ordinary farmers and craftsmen in overcoming the hardships that accompanied colonial settlement.

4. Understand the conditions which faced indentured servants and African slaves in English colonies.

5. Identify the events in European religious history which had the greatest impact on the colonial settlement of religious groups.

6. List the people and events which influenced the modern constitutional positions that exist with regard to church and state.

Identifications

Identify the following terms as you read the chapter; also note the significance of the term.

1.	primogeniture	2.	Sir Walter Raleigh
3.	George Calvert, Lord Baltimore	4.	mercantilism
5.	Elizabeth I	6.	Joint Stock Company
7.	House of Burgesses	8.	Powhatan
9.	indenture and slavery	10.	middle passage
11.	Puritans	12.	separatists and Pilgrims
13.	Mayflower Compact	14.	Massachusetts Bay Colony
15.	William Bradford	16.	John Winthrop
17.	Thomas Hooker	18.	Roger Williams
19.	Anne Hutchinson	20.	William Penn

Focus Your Reading

Employ the terms you have identified above in answering the following questions:

1. How did migrating European Aristocrats try to transplant a feudal system? Why did they fail?

2. What were Richard Hakluyt's visions concerning English trade? How do his ideas reflect mercantilism?

3. Discuss the development of the Jamestown colony from 1607 to 1624 as Unger describes it. Why does Unger think the presence of women would have made a difference?

4.   Imagine you are an African captured and sold into slavery in the 18th century. Write an account of your experiences, including the middle passage, the comparison of an indentured servant's life, and the skills brought from Africa.

Questions

Multiple Choice

1.   Which of the following doomed proprietary colonies in Virginia, Maryland and New York?
    a.   "gentlemen" refused to do manual labor
    b.   colonists did not understand the agricultural methods of Indians
    c.   several Europeans tried to set up European feudal systems
    d.   all of the above

2.   Mercantilism is best defined as:
    a.   a colonial system in which the goal is to glorify the nation using gold and silver to finance foreign wars
    b.   a system which empowers merchants to buy and sell colonial grants with stolen gold
    c.   a foreign policy which allows English merchants to outwit Spanish merchants
    d.   all of the above

3.   Virginia was named for
    a.   the wife of James I
    b.   Chief Powhatan's successor
    c.   Queen Elizabeth
    d.   the first woman born at Roanoke

4.   What caused the attack by Opechancanough's warriors at Jamestown in 1622?
    a.   the English poisoned Indian wine casks
    b.   the London Company failed to pay promised wages
    c.   the Indians didn't like the college established for them
    d.   Virginia settlers ignored Indian claims on the James River

5.   Which of the following were reasons that promoters needed involuntary immigrants?
    a.   greed
    b.   there were not enough workers to do the work
    c.   cash crop growers could not take advantage of cheap land
    d.   all of the above

6.   What part did racism play in the English colonies?
    a.   Africans were viewed as lesser beings
    b.   Africans were given the rights of servants
    c.   African women could not be exploited sexually
    d.   Africans were viewed as equals

7.   When slaves became more valuable, what was done to protect their owners?
    a.   they were viewed as "servants for life"

        b.   restrictions were placed on their movements
        c.   they became "things" under the law
        d.   all of the above

8.   The main achievement of the Pilgrims of Plymouth was
        a.   to charter the Massachusetts Bay Colony
        b.   to settle the fishing village of Salem
        c.   to set up a small colony of separatists in Cape Cod Bay
        d.   to desire to be "as a city upon a hill"

9.   How did John Winthrop's theocratic republic operate?
        a.   all adult family heads who were Puritan church members could vote
        b.   women and non-church members could not vote
        c.   the colony had 9000 inhabitants by 1640
        d.   all of the above

10.   Anne Hutchinson was declared a heretic for saying:
        a.   only a few people could preach God's word
        b.   that she knew what the Holy Spirit wanted
        c.   that the Puritan colony would be ruined by God
        d.   all of the above

11.   William Penn's "frame of government" included all by which of the following?
        a.   atheists and non-believers would be welcome in the colony
        b.   any male renter who paid taxes could vote
        c.   all taxes would be approved by the colonial legislature
        d.   there were only two crimes punishable by death: treason and murder

12.   What were the limits of toleration in the English colonies?
        a.   Catholics and Jews could worship openly in only a few places
        b.   toleration usually meant toleration within Protestant sects
        c.   several colonies had tax-supported "established" churches
        d.   all of the above

Essay

1.   Compare the aristocratic impulse with the profit motive as explanations for colonial settlement. Assess the reasons for success and failure in both cases.

2.   What was the role of indentured service in settlement and the solution of labor shortages?

3.   Why was slavery deemed to be necessary in the seventeenth century? How was it justified? Discuss some of the long-term effects of African culture and forced servitude.

4.   Compare the practice of religious toleration in the settlement of Massachusetts Bay and the Pennsylvania colony. What is the continuing influence of Puritan beliefs in American society.

5. Discuss the religious views of Roger Williams and Anne Hutchinson. What was the Puritan response to their views, and on what basis was this response made?

Map Exercises

Locate or draw in the following and expalain their significance.

1. Chesapeake Bay

2. Plymouth Colony

3. Virginia Plantation

4. Mississippi River

5. Iroquois Confederacy Territory

6. Powhatan Confederacy Territory

7. St. Augustine, Florida

8. New Amsterdam

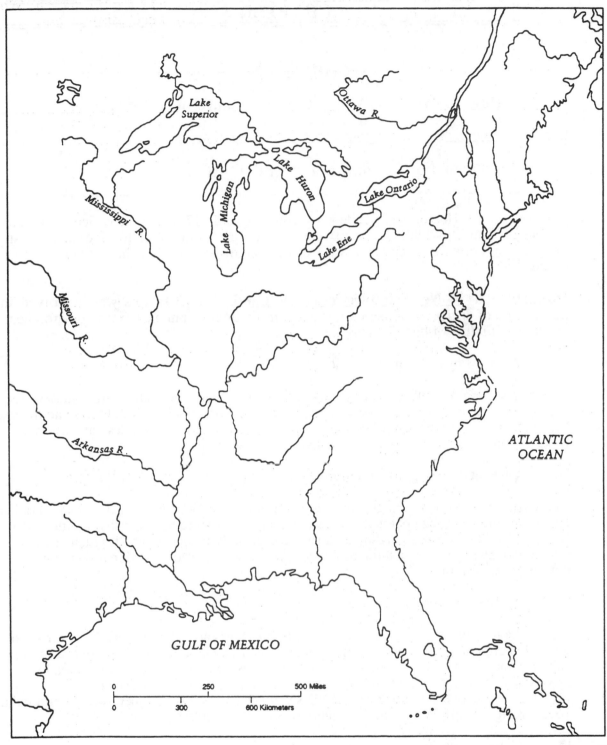

Lake Superior

Ottawa R.

Lake Michigan

Lake Huron

Lake Ontario

Lake Erie

Mississippi R.

Missouri R.

Arkansas R.

ATLANTIC OCEAN

GULF OF MEXICO

0   250   500 Miles

0   300   600 Kilometers

Map 2

17

CHAPTER 3

Colonial Society

How Did the Old World Culture Change in the Wilderness?

Summary and Outline

Summary: J. Hector St. John de Crevecoeur wrote in 1782 that the typical American was a new man, conditioned by a mixture of European customs and the vigor and industry of the New World. In what sense was Crevecoeur correct; how had this new man been created?

Outline: I. <u>A New Mixture in a New Land</u>:   Two factors were involved in the creation of distinctive American ideas and institutions: a unique physical environment and a new mixture of human beings.

A.   A New Physical Environment

America was almost entirely a wilderness in the seventeenth and eighteenth centuries: the population was confined to a narrow strip between the Appalachian Mountains and the sea. Life and travel were difficult. Such conditions shaped American attitudes: and as time went on, European settlers slowly adapted to the new environment.

B.   Diversity Among the Europeans

Crevecoeur was a French Huguenot, a member of one religious group which melted rather easily into the American population. Many other groups were not so easily assimilated; Germans and Scotch-Irish Presbyterians were especially independent. "English settlers retained many social and cultural differences which were based on regional variations within Great Britain."

C.   Native Americans

Indians and Europeans did not ordinarily mix; however early New Englanders borrowed farming techniques and plant names from the Indians, and the Indians acquired farm tools and armaments from the colonists. Aside from a few "praying Indians" converted by Reverend John Eliot, Christianity made little headway among Native Americans. Relationships between them and the settlers were generally hostile; open warfare erupted in 1672. King Philip's War as it was called, was costly to both sides.

D.   Colonial Blacks

While slaves were the main labor force on tobacco, rice and indigo plantations in the south, they usually served as laborers and craftsmen in New England and the middle colonies. West Africans brought technology and products to America; they also brought kinship networks and religious ideas. They were treated more harshly in the South than the North, and were generally denied equal access to the law in all areas. Black responses to bad treatment varied from sabotage to open rebellion. The Stono Rebellion of 1739 shocked planters in South Carolina so much that they tried to limit the hours that slaves worked to between thirteen and fifteen per day.

II. <u>Regions:</u>

A.   New England, Middle Colonies, the South

It is not as possible as it once was to separate the patterns of town settlement in New England, the middle colonies, and the colonial South. The town meetings of Puritan New England illustrated an almost ideal sense of community to earlier historians: but in the past few years new studies have shown that kinship and friendship created a similar sense of community in the Chesapeake and other regions.

B.   East—West Differences

As Europeans pushed westward they clashed with Indian tribes unwilling to surrender land to them. Eastern authorities often took up the cause of the Indians against the frontiersmen. This produced an east—west, or in Virginia, a tidewater—piedmont rivalry, in which the attempts of tidewater planters to preserve the peace were resented by piedmont farmers, such as Nathaniel Bacon, who led an unsuccessful rebellion against the Virginia governor, Sir William Berkeley, in 1675. A similar uprising occurred in Pennsylvania in 1763.

III. <u>Families:</u>   The ingredients of colonial society remained diverse, but the colonial environment continued to change European family institutions.

A.   Birth Rates, Death Rates and Family Size

The English family got larger and it became more democratic. People lived longer in America than they did in England, mainly because of low death rates and high birth rates. Early Puritan villages especially were healthy places to live, while the Chesapeake area was unhealthy. However this situation equalized itself in the eighteenth century. Young people married earlier as they had access to cheaper land than their European counterparts. Larger families were one of the outcomes.

B.   Family Roles

The family in colonial America was a little commonwealth, a political unit ruled by a father who saw to the education and behavior of his children. Mothers were responsible for household duties and childrearing. Women in general had higher status and more legal rights than their English sisters. But they were still subordinate and often resigned to a lowly position. Servants were treated and disciplined like children; children from "genteel" homes were often treated as equal members of the family.

C.   Everday Life

Housing was primitive, but generally better in town. Houses had few bedrooms, living rooms, or bathrooms. Food was plain, drink was usually beer, wine, cider or rum. Life and time were measured by the seasons.

IV.   Government: Power in the British Empire was shifting from the Crown to the people in the eighteenth century. Enlightened thinkers believed that the "popular voice" was a check on tyranny, even though "democracy" was only a remote possibility.

A.   The English Model

English government underwent two trials by fire in the seventeenth century: the Puritan Revolution and the Glorious Revolution. The result of these uprisings was to remove the absolute power of the Crown and replace it with a government ruled by parliament. The gentry in effect ruled England, but there was one law for both nobles and commoners.

B.   Colonial Political Structure

British institutions which were transplanted to the colonies included sheriffs, justices of the peace and two-house legislatures. Royal power was represented in each colony by governors, who were usually appointed, but who, as time went by, were compelled to give up financial power to their colonial assemblies. By the eighteenth century most of these bodies exercised the rights of the overseas parliament; and as a matter of fact, few limits were set on them during the era of "salutary neglect."

C.   Voters and Their Representatives

The upper houses of the colonial legislatures, usually called councils, were composed of landed gentlemen and wealthy merchants. The lower houses were elected by free white males who held property, and usually consisted of better educated squires or rising young lawyers. Town meetings in New England were also dominated by men of higher status. Though not democratic, the assemblies were very responsive to the will of the colonial citizenry.

V.   Religion: Many European religions came from Europe to the New World; but under American conditions most of them began to change.

A.   Guarding the Flame in New England

Many in the English Church came to America to escape Old World bishops; they replaced them with the New England way, a system of local self-government usually called congregationalism. The conversion of members, or "saints," was liberalized in the eighteenth century by a "covenant," which allowed New England Puritans to get involved in their own salvation.

B.   The High Church in the Wilderness

The lack of a wealthy, traditional upper class in America, which could rule a docile farming lower class, made it difficult for the Church of England to reproduce the rituals of the home country. With no bishop willing to undertake the governance of the colonial church, the organization placed religious matters in the hands of the parish. The Anglican church lost ground in the eighteenth century with most other transplanted European denominations.

C.   The Great Awakening

Mainstream religions declined; but farmers, craftsmen, and others joined in an emotional resurgence of old-time religious values called the Great Awakening. Sparked by hellfire and damnation sermons of Jonathan Edwards and the revivalism of George Whitefield, the movement presented a simple alternative to complex theology. The New Lights, as they were called, challenged the Old Lights, who remained in the formal churches.

D.   The Enlightenment

Educated people did not turn to religion so much as a new set of scientific principles, based on the rational universe of Sir Isaac Newton, called the Enlightenment. Human beings were rational. They could discover the natural laws of the universe; and human history, Enlightenment thinkers claimed, would progress as a result. Deism became a religious expression of these ideas; and it was embraced by Benjamin Franklin, Thomas Jefferson and Tom Paine, among other important leaders and writers.

VI.   Intellectual America: Intellectual development in America lagged behind the Old World.

A.   Science

Neither the social nor the physical environment of America was conducive to theoretical science; there was no laboratories or centers of learning. However, twenty-five Americans were elected to the Royal Society before 1776; and Benjamin Franklin became a world figure for his experiments in electricity.

B.   Education

The first groups to set up colonial schools were the Dutch in New Netherlands and the Massachusetts Puritans. The "Ould Deluder" law in the latter colony produced a body of literate people unique in the Western world. The foundation of Harvard College in 1636 was followed by eight more colleges before 1776. Most of these colleges emphasized both religion and the practical arts.

C.   Law and Medicine

The American colonies could not afford to support an elaborate English legal structure; so one lawyer replaced the many in the mother country. The medical profession was simplified as well; but luckily for Americans the old system of "humors" could not be easily transplanted. Colonial doctors learned their craft by day-to-day experience, observation and common sense.

VII.   The Arts: The only distinctive literary works produced in the early American colonies were histories and travel descriptions; no novels appeared, and the only poet known in her own time was Anne Bradstreet, New England's "Tenth Muse." However, newspapers, pamphlets, almanacs and practical books flourished. Music resembled an "odd noise" according to Cotton Mather. American folk songs originated in English folk music. However two composers of note, William Billings and Francis Hopkinson, appeared before 1776. Colonial painters focused on portraiture; two notable artists, John Singleton Copley and Benjamin West, migrated to Europe. American architecture was derived from European models; the best blended into the colonial environment. Innovation was limited to the practical arts and crafts.

VIII. Conclusions: Crevecoeur was correct when he asserted that America was not a carbon copy of Europe. Americans were not simply Englishmen; they were also Germans, Scotch-Irish, Indians and Africans, among others. The "new man" Crevecoeur spoke of was not yet a blend of diverse peoples; the mixing process continues to the present day.

Learning Objectives

After reading Chapter 3 you should be able to:

1. Explain what J. Hector St. John de Crevecoeur meant by the "new man" of America.

2. Understand the influence of the physical environment upon settlement patterns.

3. Identify the reasons for clashes between colonial settlers and Native Americans.

4. Explain the land and labor systems that Europeans built in the English colonies.

5. Describe the modifications in family growth and the roles of family members that took place in the colonies.

6. Compare the colonial political system with the system of the mother system.

7. Explain the changes that took place in religious life in the colonial environment, including the Great Awakening.

8. Identify the major intellectual and artistic currents of the colonial period.

Identifications

Identify the following terms as you read the chapter; also note the significance of the term.

1.	tidewater	2.	musters
3.	Chesapeake	4.	King Philip's War
5.	Bacon's Rebellion	6.	Stono Rebellion
7.	nuclear family	8.	extended families
9.	House of Burgesses	10.	proprietary colonies
11.	New England Way	12.	Half-Way Covenant
13.	Great Awakening	14.	Jonathan Edwards
15.	Enlightenment	16.	Benjamin Franklin
17.	Anne Bradstreet		

Focus Your Reading

Employ the terms you have identified above in answering the following questions:

1. Compare the exchanges of colonial Europeans and Native Americans. Discuss sources of conflict between the two groups.

2. Devise a family history based on a real or imagined ancestor who lived in either New England or the Chesapeake region in the eighteenth century. What would be the main determinant of his family size?

3. Why did traditional religions have to change their organizational structures in the New World? What effect did these changes have on social and political life?

4. Compare the Great Awakening and its impact with the intellectual movement called the Enlightenment. What were the effects of both movements?

5. Compare and contrast the economy, social structure, racial composition, family structure and place of women in the New England colonies and with the Chesapeake colonies.

Questions

Multiple Choice

1. Americans were not simply transplanted Europeans, according to Crevoeur, but they
    a. carried old habits to the new land
    b. left behind a good deal
    c. had been transformed by new circumstances
    d. all of the above

2. Eighteenth-century German immigrants tended to
    a. hold on to their old ways
    b. mix eagerly with the English-speaking majority
    c. have smaller barns than their neighbors
    d. all of the above

3. The new studies of Darrett and Anita Rutman show that the Chesapeake communities
    a. were chaotic, anomic places
    b. had a sense of community through kinship circles
    c. lacked the equivalent of a New England town meeting
    d. were completely different from the "peaceable kingdoms"

4. The policy of British Protestants toward Native Americans was
    a. to convert them to Christianity by mass baptism
    b. to intermarry with them

c. to respect their culture

d. to convert only a few who became "civilized"

5. Which Indian methods of warfare were adopted by colonists during King Philip's War?

 a. ambushes and scalping

 b. mass formation

 c. the use of bows and arrows

 d. all of the above

6. Black workers performed all of the following labors except

 a. ordained Christian ministry

 b. tobacco and rice work

 c. seamanship and assistance to craftsmen

 d. silversmithing and gunsmithing

7. In comparison to the typical size of the English family, the colonial family in New England was

 a. smaller

 b. larger

 c. about the same

 d. unstable

8. The Chesapeake was a generally unhealthy region compared to New England because

 a. malaria and dysentery attacked pregnant women

 b. tobacco cargo vessels brought in European diseases

 c. "agues" or fevers plagued the lowland rice areas

 d. all of the above

9. What advantages did a colonial American wife have over her European sisters?

 a. divorce was easier to obtain

 b. wife abusers were punished

 c. colonial widows got bigger portions of estates

 d. all of the above

10. The Glorious Revolution

 a. removed the Stuart King Charles I

 b. established democratic rule in England

 c. placed Parliament in control of laws and taxes

 d. all of the above

11. In which colonies was the governor elected by citizens?

 a. Massachusetts and New York

 b. Connecticut and Rhode Island

 c. Pennsylvania and Delaware

 d. the Carolinas

12. The first authentic American poet was

 a. George Whitefield

 b. Jonathan Edwards

 c. Anne Bradstreet

 d. Benjamin Franklin

Essay

1. Compare the treatment of American Indians and Black Africans in colonial America. Why was Christianity not seriously considered a necessity for either group?

2. What family practices that are important today seem to have their origins in the colonial period? How was the wilderness environment a factor?

3. Compare the English political and legal system to the colonial American system. Which institutions were directly adapted and which were highly modified? What were the long-term effects of such adaptations and modifications?

4. Discuss the impact of Benjamin Franklin's various contributions to colonial American societies. Was he most valuable as an inventor, a scientist, a diplomat or a journalist and writer?

Map Excercises

Locate or draw in the following and explain their significance.

<u>Colonial Claims</u>

1. Massachusetts Bay Colony

2. New York

3. Connecticut

4. Rhode Island

5. Pennsylvania

6. Virginia

7. Carolina, North and South

8. Florida, claimed by Spain

Lake Superior

Ottawa R.

Lake Huron

Lake Michigan

Lake Ontario

Mississippi R.

Missouri R.

Arkansas R.

ATLANTIC OCEAN

GULF OF MEXICO

0	250	500 Miles
0	300	600 Kilometers

Map 7

CHAPTER 4

Moving Toward Independence:

Why Did the Colonists Revolt?

Summary and Outline

Summary: Both participants in and historians of the struggle for American Independence argued about the causes of the conflict. Were they political, religious or economic? Was one cause more important than any other?

Outline: I. The Colonial Economy: Any consideration of economic causes must include the strengths and weaknesses of the colonial economy and the policies of Great Britain that influenced its growth.

A.   Agriculture

American colonial agriculture was neither efficient nor innovative; labor was scarce and new land was cheap and plentiful. New England could produce only enough foodstuffs for local use, while the middle colonies harvested large surpluses. Tobacco planting in the south had shifted to the piedmont region, leaving the tidewater to grow rice and other grain crops. Indigo and naval stores were produced in the Carolinas for overseas export.

B.   Fishing and Whaling

Cod fishing was New England's most important economic activity by the eighteenth century; whaling was also a profitable enterprise. Both of these activities provided products from the sea that could be sold for export: dried fish and whale oil.

C.   Colonial Industry

Every colonial town had its craftsmen who made barrels, wagon wheels, shoes, tools and who built homes. As towns grew, workshops became manufacturing establishments and a few even had foundries that produced iron. Every farm was a self-sufficient workshop as well. Shipbuilding was a large-scale industry in New England before 1700.

D.   Commerce

Local consumption was a major factor in the colonial economy, but foreign trade raised it above the subsistence level. Surplus grain went to the West Indies and tobacco, rice and naval stores were shipped to Europe. New England merchants earned hard cash be selling their surplus foodstuffs and wood products to Caribbean planters. Molasses and sugar obtained by this exchange could be made into rum, which in turn was traded for slaves in West Africa.

E.   Wealth and Inequality

In general the average colonist fared very well by pre-industrial standards; the exceptions were slaves and some rural farmers who did not have access to urban markets. Merchants and professional people occupied the peak of the colonial social pyramid, followed by skilled craftsmen and shopkeepers. Apprentices, journeymen and laborers occupied the lower end of the class structure. There was inequality in the cities and older rural areas, but this trend was offset by the "leveling" effect of the open frontier.

II.   Cost and Benefits of Empire Before 1763:   The British Empire was the political framework within which the colonial economy grew.

A.   The Economic Balance Sheet

Colonial merchants were restricted in their trading patterns by regulatory measures based on the theory of mercantilism: Navigation Acts to keep trading profits in English hands, lists of enumerated products which had to be shipped to London first, and limitations on colonial manufacturing. All of these provisions raised the costs of doing business for American merchants. But the cost of defending the Empire was great and for the most part necessary to the prosperity of all concerned.

B.   The Political Ledger

On balance, British rule in the American colonies was mild before 1763; the colonial assemblies had achieved a large measure of independence after the "Glorious Revolution of 1688. Parliament altered a few colonial laws and the English Board of Trade exercised little direct control during the period of "salutary neglect."

C.   The Issue of Religion

Most American colonials were Protestant Nonconformists and fearful of an Anglican church establishment in the New World; for the most part this fear was groundless.

III.   The Crisis of Empire: After 1763 the easy-going nature of the British imperial administration changed; most articulate Americans found this change intolerable.

A.   The English-French Connection

New France was established in Canada at about the same time that the English colonies were settled on the Atlantic coast. From the beginning the two groups were political competitors; the French Canadians were closer to the Indians while the English had cheaper trade goods. The Iroquois sided with the English, starting a series of conflicts in which the French and their Indian allies clashed with the Anglo-Americans on a front from Maine to Louisiana.

B.   The French and Indian War

French settlement in the Mississippi valley seemed to cut off any hopes that English colonists had of land acquisition in the west. When the French built Ft. Duquesne in western Pennsylvania in 1753, a conflict ensued that involved several European powers besides France and England. The war did not turn for the British until the Indians deserted their French allies and Quebec was captured in 1759. By the Treaty of Paris in 1763, France lost virtually all its North American territory.

C.   British-American Relations During the War

The British prohibited trade with the French during the Seven Years' War, but American vessels routinely violated such restrictions. Americans also refused to pay their share of the war's cost. Most colonies rejected the recommendations of the Albany Congress, set up to improve Indian policy during the war. After the war ended the Ottawa chief Pontiac set off an Indian uprising which drove out most of the white settlers who had crossed the Appalachian Mountains.

D.   The Proclamation of 1763

A new Tory government in England decided that tighter imperial control was needed; the Proclamation of 1763 prohibited settlement west of the Appalachians, making the region an Indian preserve until tribal claims against the Crown could be settled. Colonials were dismayed by a policy which seemed to remove them from any chance of profiting from western land settlement.

E.   Changes in British Tax Policy

The British government attempted to regulate commerce by using import duties such as the Molasses Act before 1763. But after the French were driven out the British army was still needed to defend the colonists from the Indians. Laboring under a heavy debt the British government decided to make the Americans pay the bill for their own defense. The Sugar Act of 1764 was passed to collect taxes on molasses and other items, and authorize force to stop illegal trading in the West Indies.

F.   The Stamp Act

Virginians were injured by the Proclamation of 1763; New England and the middle colonies were hurt by the Sugar Act. The Grenville government next imposed a tax on legal documents, contracts and newspapers which would unite the opposition against it. The Stamp Act, along with the Quartering Act and Currency Act, offended every colonial citizen and threatened every colonial legislature. By the time the Stamp Act Congress met in 1765, boycotts and petitions had reduced the measure to a dead letter.

G.   The Townshend Acts

The Stamp Act was repealed in 1766, but hostility soon erupted between British soldiers and the Sons of Liberty, the colonial organization formed to protest the Stamp Act. Charles Townshend, Grenville's successor, imposed a new set of duties to pay salaries of British officials, and provide for writs and customs commissioners to punish violators. Merchants set up boycotts once again, but mob action was held to a minimum. Parliament canceled the Townshend Acts in 1770.

H.   Fears for Colonial Religious Autonomy

New Englanders opposed Anglican church authority for some time, especially fearing the rumored imposition of bishops, tithes and religious tests for public office. Anglican ministers aroused further suspicion when they urged compliance with the Stamp Act and Townshend duties.

I.   Patriot Ideology

During the imperial crisis American writers began to define and justify colonial "rights."
John Dickinson's Letters from a Farmer emphasized the illegality of the collection of
internal taxes by Parliament. Others borrowed from the radical Whig writers and the
political philosopher John Locke, who had defined disobedience to tyranny as a citizen's
"natural right."

J.   Massacre in Boston

Resistance to British policies came to be regarded as a patriot's duty, especially in Boston
where redcoats had taken away American jobs. In 1770 a mob attacked a British sentry,
and nervous British soldiers fired into the crowd, killing five and wounding several others.
Massachusetts Governor Hutchinson had them arrested and moved the British garrison to
the harbor.

K.   The Gaspee Incident

On June 9, 1772, the revenue cutter Gaspee ran aground near Providence, Rhode Island,
while chasing a smuggler. That evening, several prominent patriot leaders disarmed the
crew and burned the ship to the keel. Royal officials convened a commission to find the
guilty parties, but nothing came of the effort.

L.   The Tea Act

Relative calm prevailed until 1773. The Sons of Liberty could get little support for
continuing nonimportation agreements. Americans resumed trading with the British and
drank Dutch tea. The British government attempted to correct the latter by passing the Teas
Act, which eliminated the cost of the American middlemen in British East India tea sales.
The law galvanized the patriots to action at once: Americans abstained from drinking tea,
and one group of patriots dumped a shipload of tea into Boston harbor.

M.   Intolerable Acts

In response to the "Boston Tea Party" Parliament passed the so-called Intolerable of
Coercive Acts, which closed the port of Boston and removed royal officials from American
jurisdiction. Other acts limited local governments, extended the Quartering Act, "expanded
both the boundaries of Quebec and the area open to the Catholic religion."

N.   The First Continental Congress

To provide a united response to the Intolerable Acts, delegates from all the colonies except
Georgia met in Philadelphia in September 1774, and endorsed the Suffolk Resolves. A
Continental Association was established which forbade the importation or consumption of
British goods. The Congress resolved to meet again in May of 1775 if American
grievances had not been addressed by then. This was the first American step toward
political union.

O.   Lexington and Concord

The people of Massachusetts began to arm and train themselves to defy the Intolerable Acts
directly. General Gage was just as determined to enforce them; he sent 700 men to
Lexington to arrest the patriot leaders John Hancock and Samuel Adams. Paul Revere was
dispatched be William Daves to alert them. On April 19,1775, a skirmish between Gage's

troops and seventy Minutemen took place at Lexington which resulted in the death of eight Americans. Then Gage destroyed Patriot supplies at Concord. His march back to Boston was a bloody gauntlet in which 250 British and 100 Americans lost their lives.

IV.   Conclusions: Lexington and Concord turned a political argument into a war. This came about because America had become a distinct society with its own institutions and economic practices. Americans did not free themselves from British control without considering the consequences, however. The French and Indian War was a crucial turning point which weakened American dependence on Great Britain even as it saddled the mother country with an enormous debt. The British government may have been justified in its attempt to make the colonies pay for their own defense, but it was dificult to defend the conception and execution of the laws that were supposed to bring about such a goal. These policies simply forced the Americans to begin seeing themselves as oppressed peoples who ought to be free and independent.

Learning Objectives

After reading Chapter 4, you should be able to:

1.   Describe the colonial economy and its dependence on foreign markets.

2.   Explain the class structure of colonial society.

3.   Compare the advantages with the disadvantages of doing business within the British Empire for colonial merchants.

4.   Describe French colonization in Canada and compare French colonial policy with Britain's colonial policy.

5.   Explain the causes of the French and Indian War and the reasons Britain won.

6.   Explain the reasons British colonial policy changed after the War for the Empire.

7.   Evaluate the steps by which British policies produced colonial reactions from the Stamp Act to the First Continental Congress.

8.   Assess the responsibility for Britain and the colonials in the outbreak of the Revolutionary War.

Identifications

Identify the following terms as you read the chapter; also note the significance of the term.

1.   mixed agriculture   2.   mercantilism

3.   Navigation Acts   4.   Molasses Act

5.	William Pitt the Elder	6.	Proclamation of 1763
7.	George Grenville	8.	Sugar Act
9.	Stamp Act	10.	Quartering and Currency
11.	Stamp Act Congress	12.	Sons of Liberty
13.	Charles Townsend	14.	Boston "massacre"
15.	Tea Act	16.	Intolerable Acts
17.	First Continental Congress	18.	Minutemen

Focus Your Reading

Employ the terms you have identified above in answering the following questions:

1. How would a "Tory" argue for his point of view concerning the Stamp Act, the Townshend Acts and the Tea Act? Did the British have a valid position in the debate? How would Sam Adams argue against such laws?

2. List the English laws passed between 1763 and 1775 which were intended to restrict colonial economic activity. Discuss the colonial reaction to each law. Was negotiation possible in any case.

3. Why did the war break out in Massachusetts? Discuss the First Continental Congress and compare its non-violent results with the events at Lexington and Concord six months later in April 1775.

4. Construct a scenario in which the British government acts sensibly when confronted with colonial opposition to its tax policies after 1763. Consider such alternatives as admission of the colonial legislators to Parliament, a loan arrangement to pay for colonial defense, the legalization of the West Indian rum and slave trade or any other you can think of.

Questions

Multiple Choice

1. Although Thomas Jefferson and John Adams cited other reasons, Louis Hacker quoted many people who lived at the time, declaring that the cause of the American Revolution was
   a. the economic vassalage imposed on the colonies by the British
   b. a systematic British plan to reduce Americans to slavery
   c. the British plan to establish Anglican bishops in America
   d. all of the above.

2. Commerce was important to the colonial economy because
   a. foreign buyers raised it above a subsistence level
   b. the Caribbean market absorbed surplus grain
   c. exports helped colonials pay for luxury goods
   d. all of the above

3. New England merchants made up their trade imbalances with the mother country by
   a. selling grain from the middle colonies
   b. purchasing insurance in London
   c. trading in molasses and slaves in the West Indies
   d. all of the above

4. What happened to enumerated articles under the provisions of the Navigation Acts?
   a. they had to be shipped to England before they were sold elsewhere
   b. they were subject to British taxation
   c. they had to be shipped in vessels owned by British subjects
   d. all of the above

5. For the most part measures passed by the British Parliament to restrict colonial industry
   a. were very effective
   b. had the desired effect
   c. probably had little effect
   d. discouraged Americans from buying British hats

6. Politically the main effect of the Glorious Revolution in the colonies was
   a. to encourage self-government in the colonial legislatures
   b. to arouse fears of direct royal control
   c. to deny the rights of northern colonies to tax themselves
   d. to bring representatives of absolute monarchy to power

7. What did France lose by the Treaty of Paris in 1763?
   a. all its claims in the North American continent
   b. all North American territories except Louisiana
   c. all of Canada
   d. North American territory in what is now the United States

8. American colonials did all of the following during the French and Indian War except
   a. trade flour and fish for French wines in the West Indies
   b. set up a common policy toward the Indians
   c. refuse to pay their share of the war costs
   d. delay voting money for supplies

9. The purpose of Grenville's Sugar Act was
   a. to force Americans to pay part of their own defense bill
   b. to prevent smuggling in the West Indies
   c. to set up a court to enforce all navigational acts
   d. all of the above

10. The Stamp Act was finally repealed because of
    a. mob violence
    b. petitions to Parliament

c.   economic pressure on British merchants
d.   all of the above

11.   The tea tossed into Boston Harbor by the patriots protesting the Tea Act was owned by
a.   Samuel Adams
b.   John Hancock
c.   The British East India Company
d.   American tea importers

12.   The first Continental Congress did all of the following except
a.   declare war on Great Britain
b.   condemn the Intolerable Acts
c.   urge Americans to boycott British goods
d.   attack all British trade legislation since 1763

Essay

1.   Compare the colonial economies of New England, the middle colonies and the Chesapeake region. Which area found it easiest to earn overseas credits and why? Which area had to be the most creative in maintaining its economy?

2.   Discuss the political background of the American colonies. Was the autonomy that was increasingly obtained by the colonial assemblies part of a British policy or was it the result of indifference?

3.   What was happening in the world during the eighteenth century that changed life in the American colonies after 1763? Were Americans insensitive and selfish in their reactions to British problems with the French and the Indians?

4.   Discuss Samuel Adams' role in the American Revolution including the likelihood of someone with his background becoming an American hero. What was the role of violence in the "radical" activities of the Sons of Liberty?

CHAPTER 5

The Revolution

How Did It Change America?

Summary and Outline

Summary: Many conservative Americans who favored independence from Great Britain feared that a war might turn the social structure upside down. Did the Revolution undermine values and weaken institutions in the new society?

Outline: **I. American Prospects:** Patriots and loyalists alike recoiled at the thought of independence from England in the spring of 1775. Britain had the advantage in numbers, experience in warfare and unity. On the other hand she also had enemies both in Europe and in North America, while Americans would be fighting on their own ground. Many patriots were unwilling to risk their lives and property, however; and Loyalists would cooperate with British armed forces.

A. Military Forces

There were few American military leaders with command experience on a large scale. Ordinary colonial soldiers knew how to use firearms and were experienced in Indian fighting. Their enthusiasm waned, however, after a few months fighting the redcoats. George Washington never had more than 20,000 of the 40,000 men that passed through the Continental Army. Each colony had its own army, and gunpowder and shot were in short supply. The Continental Navy consisted mainly of privateers.

B. Creating a Government

The second Continental Congress was the country's only governing body during the Revolution. It actually operated at the pleasure of thirteen colonial legislatures; and despite this limitation it created and supplied the Continental Army, established a postal service and carried out diplomatic initiatives both with the Indians and European powers.

C. Wartime Finance

The Continental Congress could not tax Americans; and since state governments were often reluctant to exercise the power, paper money was issued to pay the army, public officials and war contractors. The inflation that resulted was uncomfortable to those who endured the plummeting value of continental money, but few people depended on money wages in the rural economy of the time.

II.   The Road to Independence:

A.   Early Battles

General Gage attacked Breed's Hill in Charlestown, Massachusetts, after retreating from Lexington and Concord. American defenders were swept off the hill by regular British troops, but at the cost of one thousand redcoats. Ethan Allen had already taken Fort Ticonderoga; but Montgomery and Arnold failed to capture Quebec. Lord Dunmore's Loyalist army was overwhelmed in the South; and by March, 1776, General Howe had been forced to evacuate Boston.

B.   Turning Points

The British King rejected Congress' Olive Brance Petition and in December of 1775 declared the colonies in open rebellion, blockading American ports and making reconciliation impossible. When Lord Dunmore armed slaves in the British cause, Chesapeake planters joined the Patriot ranks. French and Spanish aid was sent. But most colonials were unwilling to make the final break with England until they read Thomas Paine's eloquent Common Sense.

C.   Independence Declared

Paine's denunciation of King George and the British government sold 120,000 copies in three months. One by one the colonial legislatures authorized their delegates in the Continental Congress to support independence. Richard Henry Lee resolved on June 7, 1776, that the United Colonies "ought to be free and independent states"; and the Congress appointed Thomas Jefferson and others to prepare a Declaration of Independence, which was formally approved on July 4. The document contained "a long train of abuses and usurpations" which were blamed on King George III: the right to overthrow such a tyrant, and the "inalienable right to life, liberty and the pursuit of happiness" borrowed from the Whig philosopher John Locke.

III.   The Fight for Independence: The people of the American colonies celebrated the Declaration of Independence. General Howe and his brother Admiral Howe offered Congress a compromise proposal, which was rejected.

A.   The War in the East, 1776-77

Washington was forced to abandon New York in 1776; he could only redeem his defeat by routing the Hessians at Trenton at year's end. He won at Princeton, New Jersey, as well; but in 1777, Philadelphia was lost to Generals Howe and Cornwallis. The most significant victory for the Continental Army in 1777 was the surrender of 6,000 British troops under "Gentleman Johnny" Burgoyne at Saratoga, New York, in October.

B.   The French Alliance

The victory at Saratoga was a signal to the French that the Americans might win their war for independence. In 1778, Benjamin Franklin and others were sent to Paris to negotiate two treaties with the Bourbon government, one guaranteeing each nation free trading rights, and a second, which pledged mutual action against Great Britain until the United States won its independence. Several northern European countries organized a League of Neutrals that isolated the English by the end of the Revolution.

C.   War in the West

The British worked diligently to befriend the Indians on the western frontier during the Revolution. The Mohawk chief Joseph Brant supported the British in New York; and during 1778 the Iroquois joined Loyalists who spread panic on the New York and Pennsylvania frontiers. The British and their Indian allies controlled the Northwest throughout the war; but the Patriots were able to reoccupy Kentucky and the Southwest.

D.   Eastern Battles, 1778-80

The British were war weary after Saratoga; the loss of American trade and the impending American alliance with France posed severe economic problems. The winter of 1777-78 was also Washington's most miserable, spent in the icy poverty of Valley Forge. The British captured Charleston, South Carolina, and were victorious at Camden. However in 1779 the last British troops were driven out of New Jersey.

E.   Victory at Yorktown

American morale was as low as 1780 in it was two years earlier. Front-line mutinies occurred in Pennsylvania and New Jersey that winter. In the fall of 1780 General Benedict Arnold went over to the British when it became known he was planning to surrender West Point to the enemy. However discouraging all of this was, final victory came for the Americans at Yorktown when General Cornwallis was cornered on the Virginia coast by Lafayette, Washington and Rochambeau in cooperation with the French Navy under Admiral de Grasse. On October 19, 1781 the British and Hessian troops surrendered .

IV.   The Articles of Confederation: In June 1776 the Continental Congress established a committee to draft a constitution for the United States that would allow the congress to conduct the Revolutionary War and provide for a permanent government after the war. The committee proposed a legislature which gave each state one vote; taxation would continue to be imposed by the states in proportion to their population. Western land boundaries proved to be a stumbling block in the original plan, so a modified plan was adopted in 1781 which established the first formal union of American States. The Confederation Congress could conduct war and foreign affairs, make treaties, borrow money and coin money and manage public lands in the West. There were no permanent executive or judicial branches; there was no Confederation power to tax, and amendments had to be passed by every state.

V.   Social Change: American Loyalists and moderate Patriots were concerned that the social order would be overthrown with the old political order. Some historians also believed the Revolution was as much a conflict over who should rule at home as it was over home rule.

A.   A Revolutionary Experience?

The world has experienced social revolutions in France in 1789 and in Russia in 1917. Did America experience an abrupt and violent overthrow of an old elite which was then replaced by new rulers who spoke for the previously oppressed? Loyalists did not qualify as an old elite, for they came from all classes; there were poor Tories and black Tories. Patriots were often from the highest and lowest portions of colonial society as well; many were rich merchants and planters. Farmers and shopkeepers were the backbone of the Continental Army. The expulsion of Loyalists and the takeover of their lands did not change the social make-up of the colonial community.

B.   Democratization

Slavery collapsed under the blows of revolution in the North, but it continued in the South, the protests of Thomas Jefferson notwithstanding. The ferment of the Revolution also improved the treatment of law breakers and the position of women. Liberalized divorce laws were passed in New England and the education of women got a boost in all the new states.

C.   New Politics

The states felt the revolutionary upheaval as well; both legislative houses became elective as did most governors. Underrepresented frontier areas were enfranchised; and in some states, all white males got the vote. Formal bills of rights were added to new state constitutions. Conventions were added as expressions of the will of the people to change governments; in a sense, "the people" became the ultimate source of power, if one excludes blacks, women, Indians and a few others.

D.   Privilege

The Revolution had a widespread effect on the remnants of European aristocratic institutions. The Anglican Church was removed from its privileged place in several states. The practices of entail and primogeniture were banned in almost all of the new states.

VI.   Making the Peace: The Americans experienced difficulties with their allies when it was time to draft a peace treaty ending the Revolutionary War. The Spanish wanted the rock of Gibraltar and the French had visions of returning to the Mississippi valley. The Rockingham administration in England hoped to restrict the Americans to areas that they controlled by arms. Benjamin Franklin, John Jay and John Adams concentrated on the English minister Oswald, and negotiated a new boundary at the Mississippi River with fishing rights in Newfoundland. The treaty of Paris was signed on September 3, 1783.

VII.   Conclusions: Americans were jubilant over their newly won independence at first, but as the smoke cleared they realized war damage had to be repaired and groups displaced by the Revolution would have to be reconciled. America did not experience a social revolution. Most of the problems the new nation faced concerned political unity.

Learning Objectives

After reading Chapter 5, you should be able to:

1.   Assess the military prospects of the British and the American colonies at the beginning of the war.

2.   Review the methods adopted to finance a wartime governing body.

3.   Describe the military strategies of the Revolution with special reference to turning points in the war.

4.   Describe the Articles of Confederation.

5.   Explain the difference between a social revolution and political revolution.

6.   Describe the political changes in the new states as compared to the colonial legislatures.

7.   Evaluate the positions of the Unites States, Great Britain and other European powers before and after the Treaty of Paris was signed.

Identifications

Identify the following terms as you read the chapter; also note the significance of the term.

1. Olive Branch Petition	2. Second Continental Congress
3. Loyalists	4. Marquis de Lafayette
5. Battle of Bunker Hill	6. Common Sense
7. John Locke	8. Saratoga
9. George Washington	10. Benedict Arnold
11. Yorktown	12. Dickinson Plan
13. Articles of Confederation	14. Molly Pitcher
15. Abigail Adams	16. Treaty of Paris

Focus Your Reading

Employ the terms you have identified above in answering the following questions:

1.   What might have happened had the British government accepted the Olive Branch petition in 1775 before the Declaration of Independence? Compare this possible situation with what might have occurred had the United States accepted Lord North's offer in 1778.

2.   Why did the British enlist slaves in their military force? Why didn't slaves enlist in the Patriot army? Why were Indians sympathetic to the British? Could either of these groups expect an improvement in their lives if the Patriots won? Why or why not?

3.   Discuss the Declaration of Independence as a propaganda tool. What were its main points? Which points were political and historically accurate? How does the Declaration compare with Common Sense?

4. Discuss the strategy of the British for suppressing the American rebellion. Why is the Battle of Saratoga considered to be the turning point of the war. Why was French aid considered essential for the American victory.

5. Discuss the American Revolution as a social revolution. Which institutions were overthrown and which were retained? Why was slavery not abolished? Why were all males not given the right to vote?

6. How did the Americans govern themselves during the war? Compare the Dickinson Plan with the Articles of Confederation.

Questions

Multiple Choice

1. All of the following were British advantages on the eve of the American Revolution except
   a. Britain was the strongest nation on Earth
   b. Britain was familiar with the terrain
   c. Britain was dominant in North America, India and elsewhere
   d. the British army was large and experienced

2. The Continental Congress lacked the power to
   a. tax
   b. issue paper money
   c. issue bonds
   d. all of the above

3. Common Sense argued that
   a. the United States should separate itself from Great Britain
   b. King George had sent redcoats, Indians, Germans and slaves to fight them
   c. monarchy was a tyrannical system condemned by God
   d. all of the above

4. Which principle in the Declaration of Independence was borrowed from the radical English Whigs?
   a. that the people could overthrow a government not based on the consent of the governed
   b. that the divine right of kings was the source of authority
   c. that property rights were more important than individual rights
   d. all of the above

5. The turning point of the Revolution for the Americans was
   a. Washington's defeat of the Hessians at Trenton
   b. the North Carolina battle with the Cherokees
   c. Burgoyne's surrender at Saratoga
   d. the ambush of General Herkimer at Oriskany

6. Which of the following was the crucial factor in the surrender of Cornwallis at Yorktown?
   a. the British navy's strategic problems
   b. French forces under Lafayette, Rochambeau and de Grasse

c. the failure of the Hessian troops
d. Benedictt Arnold's defection at West Point

7. Which of the following was <u>not</u> in the Articles of Confederation?
   a. a formal union of American states
   b. the power to conduct war and make treaties
   c. the power to coin money and issue bills of credit
   d. the power to impose taxes on citizens of the states

8. Redistribution of land and wealth during the Revolution did not constitute a social revolution, according to the author, because
   a. America was not a society of a few landlords and a landless peasantry
   b. only about half of the land in the colonies was confiscated
   c. most of the land expropriated was brought up by former Tories
   d. all of the above

9. Services performed by women in the Revolution included
   a. boycotting English goods
   b. supporting colonial families while men were fighting
   c. direct money contribution
   d. all of the above

10. All of the following changes were made by the new state governments except
    a. elected governors
    b. elected upper houses in the legislatures
    c. the vote for all male taxpayers
    d. the vote for women

11. What was the type of "mixed government" that was favored by most Patriot leaders?
    a. a government that combined both talent and numbers
    b. a government that was democratic
    c. a government that included women, blacks and Indians
    d. a government that retained hereditary privileges

12. Primogeniture was the practice of
    a. forbidding heirs to sell their inheritances
    b. preserving large land holdings for aristocrats
    c. forbidding tenant farmers from moving to new lands
    d. favoring the first-born son in inheritances

Essay

1. Compare the advantages and disadvantages of Americans in the Revolutionary War. What were the advantages and disadvantages of the British?

2. What evidence was there that the Continental Congress and the Confederation Congress that succeeded it were not given adequate powers to conduct war? Why did many Americans oppose any national government at all?

3. What was the impact of the Revolution on the rights and privileges of ordinary farmers and workers, women, Indians and slaves? Who benefited and who did not?

4.   Discuss the importance of diplomacy in the settlement that led to the Treaty of Paris in 1783. What might the United States have had for boundaries if the negotiating team sent to France had been less "hard headed"?

CHAPTER 6

The Origins of the Constitution

By Popular Demand?

Summary and Outline

Summary: Why was the Constitution written? Was it obvious to everyone that the Articles of Confederation were inadequate for the new union of states; or was the clamor aroused by a few powerful men who were so concerned with growing democratic tendencies that they demanded a stronger central government?

Outline: **I.** **America in 1780s**

A.   Agriculture

Severing political ties with England meant the end of both bounties paid to some crop growers and favored status in English markets for others. Farm prices fell while crops went unsold. Frontier farmers could not send their produce to market because the Spanish would not allow Americans to use New Orleans for such a purpose.

B.   Commerce

American shippers moved enthusiastically into overseas trading unhampered by British navigation laws; but new trade routes could not compensate for the loss of British imperial markets. American navigation acts were suggested to keep British vessels from competing in American coastal trade.

C.   Industry

With the return of peace American consumers went on a spending spree for British goods, putting local manufacturers out of work. Artisans demanded that the states enact protective tariffs which would raise the prices of imported goods. Unfortunately such measures produced trade wars among the states which nullified the advantages of a continental trading area.

D.   Creditors and Debtors

Unable to impose taxes, the Confederation Congress stopped paying off the national debt. Government securities dropped in price and were bought up by speculators, who also bought up state securities. Hard currency became scarce; deflation hurt farmers, artisans and debtors. Many debtors demanded that the states issue paper money; creditors, of course, recoiled at such measures. The economic crisis was genuine, and most Americans blamed the weak confederation government.

E.	Confederation Finances

The Confederation Congress could not pay its soldiers, creditors or security holders because it had no financial resources. States had the same problems and could not send much money to relieve the national crisis. The Congress had to borrow money from foreign sources and sell western land. Attempts to raise a duty on all incoming goods to pay the defaulted debt foundered when the unanimous consent of all the states could not be mustered.

F.	Nationalism

Americans declared their independence from Europe in many ways during the confederation period: by establishing separate churches, their own academies of the arts and sciences, their own standards and even their own history. When new nationalists looked around them, however, they could only see weakness and humiliation; a Confederation Congress that was "abused, laughed at and cursed in every company."

**II.	Foreign Affairs:**	If the Confederation government was regarded as weak and the object of derision at home, in the words of Thomas Jefferson, respect for the government was "annihilated" abroad. The British refused to vacate forts and trading posts on American soil until Loyalists were compensated and prewar debts were paid. Spain not only closed the Mississippi to American farmers, but refused to allow trading in Latin American ports. John Jay negotiated trade concessions with the Spanish and agreed to forego the right of deposit in New Orleans for twenty-five years. Westerners protested and the treaty was not ratified in Congress. The American Navy was unable to protect commercial shipping from North African pirates.

**III.	The Public Domain:**	The Confederation government handled itself well in regard to the administration of public lands; after 1784 it possessed almost a quarter of a billion acres in the Ohio Valley. The decision as to how this land should be disposed of and how it would be governed was crucial to the future of the nation.

A.	The Land Ordinance of 1785

In 1785 Congress decided to steer a middle course between the New England method of orderly land development and the Southern system of open choice. All government lands were to be divided into surveyed townships and sections, half of which would be sold in small 640-acre parcels, and half of which would be auctioned off in tracts of 23,000 acres.

B.	Congress's Indian Policy

Congress's record in dealing with Indians matched its lack of success in foreign affairs. Agreements were negotiated with Iroquois and several other tribal groups in 1784. But the treaties broke down when renegade white settlers from the West moved into the Ohio Valley. The Indians declared the whole valley closed to white settlement. As a result of this catastrophe and others, many Americans lost confidence in the Confederation government.

C.	The Ordinance of 1787

One major accomplishment cannot be taken away from the Confederation: the Northwest Ordinance, which provided a government for the Ohio Valley until the area should enter the Union as separate states. The ordinance mandated that the territory should be organized into three to five states, should be free of slavery, and could set up new state governments when 60,000 inhabitants submitted a constitution to Congress. Americans could now leave their old states and go west, in full knowledge that they would not have to give up their political privileges.

IV. **The Constitutional Convention:** By 1785 it was clear to many Americans, not just a small group of powerful men, that the nation needed more effective central government. The process of revising the Articles of Confederation would be a long and arduous one; it was not until 1786 that five states would meet in Annapolis, Maryland, to discuss commercial problems. A full-scale convention to discuss fundamental changes would not be planned until May 1787.

A. Shays' Rebellion

Congress was a moribund institution until the summer of 1786 when it was awakened by events in Massachusetts. High taxes in that state which were levied to pay the war debt provoked discontent among western farmers who were burdened by legal fees. Hoping to end foreclosures for debt default and unpaid taxes., they formed a military drilling team under Daniel Shays. Governor Bowdoin raised a militia with private money and dispersed the rebels in January 1787. Small as it was, the uprising convinced nationalists that a constitutional convention was overdue.

B. The Challenge

The meeting convened at Independence Hall in Philadelphia on May 14, 1787, was an assembly of giants, capable and important men, who had the confidence of the citizens who sent them. They invented a new governmental form, a written constitution, which drew upon the English experience and the traditions of the thirteen colonies. The "Founding Fathers" added to this background a historical understanding of the ancient institutions of Rome and contemporary thought of the European Enlightenment. They were men of experience who wanted a strong central government that balanced personal liberty with respect for private property , Conflicts arose between the champions of all points of view represented in the various states; compromise as a result was inevitable.

C. The Debate on Representation

Acting for James Madison, Edmund Randolph submitted the Virginia Plan, a completely new government with separate legislative, executive and judicial departments. The Congress would have two houses, elected by the states in proportion to their population. The new government would confer broad powers on the central government. This was countered by William Patterson's New Jersey Plan which gave equal representation to each state regardless of population. It granted the power to tax and regulate commerce to the national government sharing powers with the states. A debate followed between advocates of the two plans: on the whole the plan for a strong central government prevailed. But the Senate would represent all states equally, while the House of Representatives would be elected by the stakes in proportion to their population. When the convention tried to settle upon what the population was, slaves and taxation became sensitive issues. Finally it was decided that both taxes and representation would be based on "the whole number of free persons" and "three-fifths of all other persons." Slaves were treated as property and as three fifths of a person.

D. Freedom or Order

Most of the convention delegates favored both representation on a broad basis and some provision for order and rule by the "best men." Following the Enlightenment philosopher

Montesquieu, they adopted the idea of checks and balances among the three branches of government. A chief executive could veto acts of Congress, but he could be overridden by a two-thirds vote. He would command the armed forces, but only Congress could declare war. His appointments would have to be confirmed by the Senate. Although it is not stated in the Constitution, legal scholars believe the federal courts have the power to declare acts of Congress invalid. The Supreme Court would be appointed with a host of other officers in each branch. Such "aristocratic" features were offset by "popular" control in the House of Representatives.

E.   Powers of the New Government

The new national government superseded the powers of the states, fusing the nation into a single legal whole, which could now impose and collect taxes, control and regulate foreign and interstate commerce, coin money, establish a postal system, build postal roads and naturalize citizens. It could also make all laws which were deemed necessary and proper for carrying out its enumerated powers. The constitution created a federal government which left the states many responsibilities in education, law enforcement, and domestic relations. After heated arguments the document was approved on September 17, 1787.

V.   Ratification: There has been some debate among scholars as to how formidable the opposition to the Constitution was. There is no doubt that the opposition fought hard against it; but it seems clear that the federalists won the struggle for ratification with relative ease. Nine states had to adopt the Constitution before it became the Law of the Land; Delaware, Pennsylvania and New Jersey approved it quickly in 1787, while Georgia and Connecticut followed in early 1788. Massachusetts balked at the lack of a Bill of Rights, but approved when the first nine amendments were proposed by John Hancock. Following Rhode Island's rejection, Maryland and South Carolina joined the adoption states in April and May, 1788. New Hampshire was the ninth state to approve, but New York and Virginia were still to be heard from. Patrick Henry's eloquence could not halt adoption in Virginia; Alexander Hamilton and his Federalist Papers, composed with Madison and Jay, carried the day in New York. Only Rhode Island and North Carolina did not vote in the national elections if 1789. However they ratified the document after the Bill of Rights was formally added.

VI.   Conclusions: Between the end of the Revolution in 1781 and the inauguration of George Washington in 1789, Americans suffered a deteriorating economy and foreign humiliation. As a result most citizens approved of the stronger government that was created by the Constitutional Convention in Philadelphia.

Learning Objectives

After reading Chapter 6, you should be able to:

1.   Outline the principal arguments in the debate concerning the origins of the Constitution as they were presented by John Fiske and Charles A. Beard.

2.   Compare the strengths and weaknesses of the Articles of Confederation government.

3.   Contrast the political with the economic problems of the 1780's.

4. Explain the accomplishments of the Confederation government in land policy and territorial government.

5. Account for the movement to convene the Constitutional Convention.

6. Compare the two plans for representation considered by the convention.

7. Analyze the principals utilized to make the Constitution work.

8. Describe the ratification process and explain why it succeeded.

Identifications

Identify the following terms as you read the chapter; also note the significance of the term.

1. deflation
2. right of deposit
3. Land Ordinance of 1785
4. Northwest Ordinance
5. Shays' Rebellion
6. Virginia Plan
7. New Jersey Plan
8. three-fifths compromise
9. checks and balances
10. Alexander Hamilton
11. Gouverneur Morris
12. federalists
13. anti federalist
14. Federalist Papers
15. Bill of Rights

Focus Your Reading

Employ the terms you have identified above in answering the following questions:

1. Discuss the problems in the new country during the 1780s, while it was governed by the Articles of Confederation. What economic and social problems illustrated the weaknesses of the Articles?

2. Compare the Constitution with the Articles of Confederation. Include a discussion of the branches of government and how they offer a balance to too much democracy.

3. What would have happened if slavery had been abolished by the Constitution in the late eighteenth century? How would this decision have changed the South, industrial development and the conflicts which led to the Civil War?

Questions

Multiple Choice

1. All of the following were problems facing American agriculture in the 1780s except
   a. war damage
   b. severe drought
   c. loss of British subsidies
   d. loss of British markets

2. Why were city "manufacturers," artisans and craftspeople out of work immediately following the Revolution?
   a. American buyers preferred British products
   b. the war had destroyed the shops used by city craftspeople
   c. American craftspeople were incompetent
   d. all of the above

3. Which of the following was the Confederation Congress unable to pay?
   a. Revolutionary soldiers
   b. security holders
   c. government creditors
   d. all of the above

4. The right of Americans to unload Mississippi River cargo and place it on oceangoing ships was called
   a. the pursuit of happiness
   b. the right of commerce
   c. the right of deposit
   d. the respect for commerce

5. The Northwest Ordinance of 1787 was important because it
   a. excluded slavery in the territory north of the Ohio River
   b. established the principle that new states would be equal to the original states
   c. provided for territorial governors and judges before statehood
   d. all of the above

6. Shays' Rebellion frightened people for all of the following reasons except
   a. Shay was successful in getting farmers' tax bills canceled
   b. Conservatives believed that it anticipated social revolution
   c. many thought that all debts would be canceled as a result
   d. it revealed the weakness of the country for all the world to see

7. The Founding Fathers relied on all the following traditions and experiences except
   a. the ancient laws and institutions of Rome
   b. the common law tradition of England
   c. practical experience in colonial government
   d. the governing traditions of the Old Testament

8. Which of the following clashes did not take place during the Constitutional convention?

    a.   large states vs. small states
    b.   slave states vs. free states
    c.   capital vs. labor
    d.   democrats vs. aristocrats

9. The three-fifths compromise
    a.   allowed southerners three-fifths of one vote to every northern vote
    b.   limited the amount of alcohol served to Indians
    c.   counted every slave as three-fifths of a white voter
    d.   treated a slave both as property and as three-fifths of a person

10. All of the following provisions of the Constitution are examples of mixing democratic and aristocratic methods except
    a.   the choice of the President by an electoral college
    b.   Senators would be selected by state legislators
    c.   the chief executive could veto acts of Congress
    d.   Senators would have six-year terms

11. The power reserved by the Constitution to the national government to make all laws necessary and proper for executing its "foregoing powers" was called
    a.   full faith and credit
    b.   a way to check "the mob"
    c.   high crimes and misdemeanors
    d.   the elastic clause

12. One reason the Constitution was ratified was the articulate defense made of the document in
    a.   the Federalist Papers
    b.   the Bill of Rights
    c.   Rhode Island
    d.   Patrick Henry's speech

Essay

1. Discuss the creditor-debtor problem as it related to Confederation finances. Was the Constitution in any way related to the problem, as Charles Beard claimed in his Economic Interpretation of the Constitution?

2. Discuss the compromises at the Constitutional Convention, especially in the areas of shared power between large and small states and the three-fifths compromise.

3. Discuss the life of Daniel Shays. Analyze the tax laws that brought him and his fellow farmers to the point of rebellion. Why was there a radical party in Massachusetts from the pre-revolutionary days to the Constitution?

4. What happened to the unanimity one finds in the Federalist Papers after the Constitution was ratified?

CHAPTER 7

The First Party System

What Issues Divided the New Nation?

Summary and Outline

Summary: The founders did not conceive of a party system. They hoped that offices in the national government would be filled by disinterested public servants and not by men divided into factions who would seek office for selfish reasons. Yet two great parties emerged within ten years of the Constitution's adoption. What were the circumstances in which the parties developed? Were they the results of ideology? Were they planned? Or, were they formed by the followers of ambitious individuals?

Outline: I. The New Government Launched

A.   National Finances

The earliest measures passed by the Congress elected in 1789 were the Tariff Act and the Tonnage Act. The latter revealed some sectional differences, but the debates were relatively calm until the unpaid war debts were discussed in the second session. The debt was held by veterans, patriotic lenders and speculators.

B.   Hamilton's Plan for America

Alexander Hamilton of New York, the secretary of the treasury, hoped to use his new office to make the country strong and prosperous. His goal was to change the United States from a food and fiber producer to a manufacturing country like England. He incorporated his vision for the future into three reports submitted to Congress in 1790 and 1791. The First Report on Public Credit recommended assumption of all outstanding debts, so that the funded debt could be used as "an engine of business." He also proposed a federally chartered National Bank to issue bank notes, and a tariff to support "infant industries."

C.   Enacting the Hamilton Program

James Madison opposed the Funding Act of 1790, which converted both national and state debts to federal bonds at face value. Madison reflected the Southern view that Hamilton's Funding Act benefited the business interests of the North at the expense of agriculture. A compromise was offered by Thomas Jefferson which got the bill passed in exchange for a new national capital in the South. Madison opposed the bank bills as well; but Congress chartered the Bank of the United States for twenty years as the main federal depository. It was also the institution that would issue paper currency. President Washington signed the bill into law in 1791.

II.   The Beginning of Parties:

A.   The Economic Division

Hamilton's financial program drove a wedge between emerging Federalists, who were merchants, manufacturers and speculators, and emerging Republicans, who were small farmers and southern planters.

B.   The Ideological Division

There were ideological differences between Federalists and Republicans based on attitudes toward human nature, majority rule and the role of government. Republicans like Madison, Jefferson and others deplored excessive government power and distrusted manufacturers. As "agrarians" they distrusted money lending and "stock-jobbing" and favored conservation of farms and forests. Republicans tended to trust human nature while Federalists feared the rule of the "mob." However the leaders of both parties tended to be members of an elite class based on talent and achievement.

C.   The Role of Religion

Americans of the early republic admired the Republicans but voted for the Federalist party because that party was associated with the new national government and the Constitution. The Federalist program was enacted quickly, assisted by the support of President Washington. Members of established churches, Episcopalians and Congregationalists, also supported the Federal program. Baptists, Methodists, Roman Catholics and non-believers preferred the Republicans. Members of such diverse groups were often discriminated against in states dominated by traditional religions.

III.   Relations With Europe: Political parties responded not only to domestic economic and social attitudes, but also to problems that the United States faced in dealing with Europeans. England, Spain and even France often denied America the respect due an independent nation.

A.   Revolution in France

The French Revolution of 1789 proved to be a divisive political event that would further separate Federalists and Republicans. At first all Americans rejoiced in the fall of the Bourbon regime; but the Reign of Terror and the revolutionary government's attack on the church frightened many Federalists. Republicans tended to stand by the Revolutionaries even after they went to war with England, Spain, and Holland.

B.   Citizen Genet

The new French government sent Edmond Genet to ask for American aid; Jefferson favored receiving him, while Hamilton believed he would compromise the country's position in the European conflict. For his part, Genet began passing out contracts to privateers and threatened to go directly to the American people and ask for aid. Even Jefferson asked him to leave; but Genet could not return to France when a new government took power.

C.   The Partisan Press

The Genet controversy propelled the party conflict to new heights; Federalist and Republican newspapers printed scathing indictments of their enemies. Fenno's Gazette called Republicans Jacobins, or French radicals, while Freneau's National Gazette denounced the Federalists as monarchist. Jefferson finally resigned from Washington's cabinet, but continued as Republican leader.

D.   Relations with England

The European war brought the new government close to a serious breach with England over the rights of neutrals. The British objected to American commerce with France, especially the shipment of contraband through the British blockade. The British found the resulting American prosperity doubly offensive; British sailors who deserted to the American maritime fleet were often taken back by British men-of-war. "Impressment," as it was called, outraged Americans, but fear of provoking war with the British tempered such reactions.

E.   The British and the Indians

Not only did Great Britain refuse to vacate forts in the northwest United Stares, but their agents encouraged Indian tribal groups to demand a buffer state in Ohio. Washington sent General Anthony Wayne to remove the Indians as a menace to westward expansion of 1794 at the Battle of Fallen Timbers.

F.   The Jay Treaty

By the fall of 1793, 250 American ships had been confiscated by English naval commanders who were attempting to halt American trading in the French West Indies. War seemed to be a distant possibility until Chief Justice John Jay was sent to London to negotiate on the northwest forts and American trade rights. The Jay Treaty was generous to the British and labeled a sellout by the Republicans. They organized the first opposition party caucus in the House of Representatives to fight the treaty.

G.   The Whiskey Rebellion; The Pinckney Treaty

The Indians signed the Treaty of Greenville in 1795, opening up all of Ohio to pioneer farmers except for a strip along Lake Erie; two new states, Kentucky and Tennessee, were admitted into the Union in 1796. Frontier farmers in western Pennsylvania converted their grain to whiskey on order to avoid high transportation costs. However when the federal government imposed a tax on the whiskey to raise money for Hamilton's Funding Bill, the farmers rebelled, closing down federal courts and attacking federal troops who guarded the tax collector. Washington sent the militia to disperse the rebels; only two were tried for treason. The government acted with dispatch; when westerners threatened to take matters into their own hands in regard to Spain's refusal of deposit in New Orleans, Thomas Pinckney was sent to Madrid to settle that problem with equal speed. The Mississippi River was opened to free navigation as a result, and the right of deposit granted at New Orleans for three years.

H.   Washington's Farewell

Washington's "Farewell Address" in 1796 was not only a warning against entangling alliances but also a plea for national unity. His retirement deprived the Federalists of their main political asset.

I.   The Election of 1796

There was as yet only a primitive party structure at the National level. Thomas Jefferson was the Republican candidate for president; he was opposed by Vice President John Adams for the moderate Federalists and Thomas Pinckney, who was nominated by the High

Federalists. The Federalists won the electoral college, but could not coordinate their votes among the electors. Adams was chosen president and Jefferson, vice president.

J.   The XYZ Affair.

The French Directory considered the Jay Treaty an Anglo-American alliance; John Adams' presidency seemed to confirm America's pro-British stand. France refused to receive the American ambassador, Charles Pinckney, and carriedon a campaign of impressment against the American navy. Adams sent Pinckney and two others to negotiate with the French minister, Talleyrand, who in turn assigned three agents, X, Y, and Z, to demand bribery payments, loan money and a public apology from President Adams. Pinckney and the others refused, but the bad feelings set off a naval war between the United States and France that did not end until 1800. In the meantime, American forces were overthrown on the island of Hispaniola.

IV.   Republican Triumph: The concept of a loyal opposition came slowly to the United States; "men of both parties" equated political opposition with disloyalty or treason.

A.   Alien and Sedition Acts

In 1798, the Federalist-controlled Congress passed four laws known as the Alien and Sedition Acts. The Naturalization Act extended the residence requirement for citizenship from five to fourteen years, mainly to keep recent Irish and French immigrants from voting for the Republicans. The Alien Act gave the president the power to expel dangerous aliens from the country. Under the Alien Enemies Act, he could arrest, imprison or expel enemy aliens in wartime. The Sedition Act made it illegal to criticize the acts of the federal government and the president or to impede the acts of a federal officer. Secretary of State Pinckney prosecuted four Republican newspaper editors under the act. This was a political blunder as it rallied wavering Republicans back to the fold. Jefferson and Madison used the Virginia and Kentucky resolutions to voice their protest against the Federalist attack on civil liberties and free speech.

B.   The Transfer of Power

When the 1800 presidential campaign opened, the Federalists seemed to be ahead. However Washington's death and an open breach between Adams and Hamilton   reduced their chances. The Federalists nominated John Adams and Charles Pinckney while the Republicans chose Thomas Jefferson and Aaron Burr. For the first time printed party tickets and public speeches were employed. The election was thrown into the House of Representatives, and by a close vote, Jefferson was chosen third president of the United States. An orderly transfer of power took place which put the Republicans in power for the first time.

V.   Conclusions: Ten years after the ratification of the Constitution, Americans laid the foundations of a modern two-party system. Parties developed out of disagreements over Alexander Hamilton's plans for a solvent country committed to both industry and agriculture. The French Revolution divided people even further. The Federalists tended to favor broad construction of the Constitution while the Republicans favored a stricter "states rights" view. Neither party had a complete view of the nation's future; the Federalists were fearful about the possibility of democracy, while the Republicans were limited in their vision of economic growth.

Learning Objectives

After reading Chapter 7, you should be able to:

1.   Explain the attitude of the Founding Fathers concerning factions or political parties.

2.   Summarize Alexander Hamilton's proposals for establishing public credit, a national bank and protection for industries.

3.   Analyze the economic and ideological differences between the Federalists and Republicans that led to the development of the first two-party system.

4.   Explain the difficulties that the new nation experienced as a result of the French Revolution.

5.   Review the diplomatic problems with Great Britain and Spain that resulted in the Jay and Pinckney Treaties.

6.   Summarize the laws contained in the Alien and Sedition Acts.

7.   Account for the continuing struggle between governmental authority and civil liberties following the passage of the Virginia and Kentucky resolutions.

8.   Explain the significance of the elections of 1796 and 1800.

Identifications

Identify the following terms as you read the chapter; also note the significance of the term.

1. Thomas Jefferson	2. Democratic-Republican
3. Alexander Hamilton	4. First Report on Public Credit
5. Report on a National Bank	6. Report on Manufactures
7. loose construction	8. strict construction
9. Citizen Genet	10. impressment
11. Jay's Treaty	12. Whiskey Rebellion
13. Farewell Address	14. High Federalists
15. Charles C. Pinckney	16. Charles Talleyrand
17. X, Y, Z Affair	18. Alien and Sedition Acts
19. Virginia and Kentucky resolutions	

Focus Your Reading

Employ the terms you have identified above in answering the following questions:

1. To what extent was Alexander Hamilton a visionary and Thomas Jefferson an obstructionist? Which Hamiltonian doctrines would certain groups agree with today and which Jeffersonian ideas seem relevant?

2. Explain what happened to America's special relationship with France during their Revolution. Despite all the problems on the frontier, was England a more "natural" ally? Why or why not?

3. Compare and contrast Hamilton's and Jefferson's ideas about economy, international allies and ability of people to govern themselves. How do their differences influence the development of political parties?

4. Discuss the nation's attempt to deal with England, France, Spain, Indians and rebellious farmers in Pennsylvania.

Questions

Multiple Choice

1. The opinion of the delegates to the Constitutional Convention concerning political parties was
   a. that such organizations were essential to modern government
   b. that most people in America would belong to one party
   c. that factions grouped themselves around political leaders for selfish reasons
   d. that parties should be based on sound ideology

2. Hamilton wanted the federal government to assume both the national and state debts in order to
   a. establish the credibility of the new government abroad
   b. attach the interests of the rich and powerful to the nation's interests
   c. stimulate commerce and provide investment capital
   d. all of the above

3. James Madison argued against the Funding Act of 1790 because
   a. it burdened the South with taxes to redeem the debts of Northern states
   b. he believed that it favored speculators at the expense of original bond holders
   c. the act aided commercial interests at the expense of planters.
   d. all of the above

4. Congress's attitude toward Hamilton's Bank of the United States was
   a. to charter the bank with Washington's approval
   b. to turn down the Bank Bill
   c. to pass the Bank Bill over Washington's veto

d.   to discuss the idea but not to vote on it

5.   The impetus to divide early American voters into two political groups was
       a.   economic
       b.   ideological
       c.   geographical
       d.   all of the above

6.   Most Americans received the news of the French Revolution with
       a.   fear and anxiety
       b.   disdain
       c.   enthusiasm
       d.   honest criticism

7.   Citizens Genet's original purpose in coming to America was
       a.   to convince the Washington administration to declare war on England
       b.   to obtain American aid for the new government
       c.   to try to convince the Republicans to support his cause
       d.   to plot against the American government

8.   British relations with the Washington government deteriorated because
       a.   Americans were trading "illegally" with France
       b.   Americans were profiting from wartime trading activities
       c.   the British stopped American ships to search for deserters
       d.   all of the above

9.   Jay's Treaty to settle several long-standing problems with the British both on the
       sea and in the American Northwest was
       a.   well received by most Americans
       b.   a triumph of diplomacy
       c.   denounced by Republicans
       d.   favorable to the French

10.   Charles Pinckney's reply to the XYZ Commissioner's request for a bribe in 1797
       was
       a.   "millions for defense, but not one cent for tribute"
       b.   "no, no, not a six-pence"
       c.   'not now, but later"
       d.   "I'll take it up with the President"

11.   Four leading newspaper editors were prosecuted by Secretary of State, Timothy
       Pickering under the provisions of
       a.   the Sedition Act
       b.   the Alien Act
       c.   the Constitution
       d.   the principle of nullification

12.   The Virginia and Kentucky Resolutions
       a.   attacked the Alien and Sedition Acts
       b.   were written by Madison and Jefferson
       c.   claimed the right of a state to protect its people from unconstitutional federal
              laws.
       d.   all of the above

Essay

1. Discuss the formation of a two-party system in the early Republic. Were the main forces that split voters economic, ideological or geographical? Justify your choice.

2. What portions of Hamilton's financial program for the early Republic were vital to its survival and progress and which were either not needed or unnecessary? Justify your opinion based on modern problems.

3. What were the problems that Washington and Adams had with France?

4. Compare the Jay and Pinckney Treaties. Why was it easier to deal with Spain than England? How important was the political response to both treaties?

CHAPTER 8

The Jeffersonians in Office

How Did Power Affect Republican Ideology?

Summary and Outline

Summary: In 1815, President James Madison, heir to the Republican mantle of Thomas Jefferson, recommended a protective tariff, federal money for roads and canals and a national academy of learning. What had happened to strict construction in the preceding decade? Why were Republicans now Nationalists? What happened to the Federalists?

Outline: **I. President Jefferson:**   When Thomas Jefferson became president in 1800, he proved to be remarkably adaptable, declaring in his inaugural speech: "We are all Republicans, we are all Federalists."

A.   A New Republican Spirit

Jefferson was conciliatory, but he was still a Republican in his informality as new host of the executive mansion. He often served food himself, dazzling dinner companions with legislative and diplomatic requests they were unable to refuse.

B.   Federalist Legislation Repealed

Only a few new bills were passed in Jefferson's first term. He asked his Secretary of the Treasury, Albert Gallatin, to reduce the national debt by scaling down army and navy appropriations. Taxes were also reduced as large revenues came to the treasury from expanded foreign trade. Some of the Alien and Sedition Acts were repealed. Republicans were pardoned who had been imprisoned for sedition; and the Bank of the United States charter expired in 1811.

C.   A Strong Executive

Jefferson decided he could not worry about constitutional theory if he wanted to get the job done. He believed that he had to be pragmatic about rewarding office seekers as well, so almost 200 Federalists were replaced with Republicans.

D.   An Attack on the Judiciary

As the result of the Judiciary Act of 1801, the Federalists were able to fill many open judicial positions the evening before Jefferson's inauguration. To keep the new appointees from taking office, Secretary of State Madison refused to deliver their commissions while a new Judiciary Act was passed in 1802. Chief Justice John Marshall settled the matter while establishing the Supreme Court's right of judicial review, when Federalist nominee,

William Marbury was denied his commission in 1803 on grounds that the law of 1801 was unconstitutional. John Randolph of Roanoke could not convince the Senate that Samuel Chase, a Federalist Supreme Court Justice, should be removed.

II.   International Politics and Republican Policy: The need to deal effectively with foreign powers convinced Jefferson and Madison that the Federalist principle of strong central government gave the executive more authority in such matters.

A.   Jefferson Buys Louisiana

When Napoleon came to power in France in 1799, he got control of Louisiana from Spain. Jefferson became concerned that commerce on the Mississippi River and deposit at New Orleans would be closed to Americans by the French, forcing a closed alliance with England. Napoleon's plans to re-establish a North American empire in Haiti went awry, rendering Louisiana worthless to France. Jefferson sent Robert Livingston and James Monroe to Paris to purchase New Orleans and West Florida. They were unexpectedly offered the entire Louisiana territory for $15 million. Jefferson worried that the offer was unconstitutional, but he swallowed his misgivings and pushed a purchase treaty through the Senate. On December 20, 1803, Louisiana, almost equal in size to the United States, became American territory.

B.   The Lewis and Clark Expedition

Jefferson recruited his private secretary, Meriwether Lewis, and William Clark to explore the Louisiana territory, and "observe flora and fauna" and to estimate its commercial possibilities. They arrived at the Pacific Ocean in 1805 after discovering several passes through the Rockies, laying groundwork for the settlement of the continent.

C.   The Wilkinson-Burr Conspiracy

The Louisiana Purchase ended the shipping difficulties of western farmers on the Mississippi River through New Orleans, but many westerners still did not trust the government. In a scheme to detach the West from the United States, Aaron Burr conspired with General James Wilkinson and the British minister in Washington. Burr was acquitted of treason but convicted of espionage.

D.   Neutral Rights Once More

After 1803, the United States once more was caught in the middle of a dispute between England and France. The British admiralty court declared French West Indian products to be contraband which could be confiscated if carried on American ships. Napoleon retaliated with decrees that made ships with British clearances subject to French seizure. Jefferson chose not to invoke a Non-importation Act passed by Congress in 1806.

E.   The Chesapeake-Leopard Affair

Vice Admiral Sir George Berkeley, who commanded the British fleet in Nova Scotia, ordered the boarding of the U.S.S. Chesapeake in 1807, to remove a deserter named Jenkin Ratfoed. When Commodore James Barron protested the H.M.S. Leopard's action three of his sailors were killed and eighteen wounded. Americans were outraged by an unprecedented insult to their national sovereignty and began talking seriously of war with Great Britain.

F.   The Embargo

The British did not make reparation for the <u>Chesapeake</u> affair until 1811. Meanwhile war fever cooled as Jefferson pondered the military weakness of his nation. Perhaps economic warfare would bring England around. In 1807, Jefferson asked Congress to place an embargo on all exports, effectively sealing off the country from foreign trade. However so many shippers violated the embargo that an Enforcement Act was added in 1809. Popular opposition grew as the docks were deserted; Jefferson was compelled to repeal the embargo before he left office.

G.   Madison Takes the Helm

Jefferson underestimated the accomplishments of his two terms in office; he was not only able to double the size of the country but also provide a more democratic presidency. James Madison in comparison was irresolute and often wrong-headed. He was tricked by Napoleon into reimposing trade restrictions on the British when the intent of Congress was to remove all commercial impediments to American trade.

H.   Further Western Troubles

Western Americans believed that the British were still stirring up trouble among the Indians, even though Americans were causing most of the problems themselves. William Henry Harrison forced many tribes in Indiana to cede millions of acres of land, provoking the Shawnee Chief Tecumseh and his brother, "the prophet" to revive Pontiac's scheme of driving the whites out of the Mississippi Valley. Tecumseh's young followers met Harrison at Tippecanoe on the Wabash River in 1811. Westerners were also distressed by low grain prices in Europe, which they blamed on the British. War Hawks in Congress elected one of their number to the speakership.

I.   Congress Votes for War

As a result of Madison's reimposition of the embargo, British cruisers gathered off the Atlantic coast, stopping more vessels and taking suspected deserters away in droves. The British economy finally felt the pinch caused by the embargo, but Lord Castlereagh's decision to withdraw the British order imposing impressment could not be communicated to Madison and Congress quickly enough to avoid an American declaration of war in June of 1812.

J.   Who Wanted War?

Those who wanted war with Great Britain included interior New Englanders, Pennsylvanians and most Southerners and Westerners. Coastal New Englanders and New Yorkers opposed the war. Pocketbook considerations outweighed geographical location, however; the Republicans had been spoiling for a fight with the British since the embargo. Moreover national feeling had been deeply offended by orders in council, impressment. confiscation of ships, and Indian incitement.

III.   The War of 1812:   Owing in part to Republican policies, American military and naval forces were not prepared for war in 1812. There were only 6700 men in the regular army; and New England refused to send its well-trained militia. There were sixteen naval vessels but only seven were seaworthy. The Bank of the United States was not rechartered in 1811, so the treasury was bare. There were almost no roads crossing the

Appalachian mountains; the Great Lakes were useful to the war effort, but they were not connected to any major population centers.

A.   The Hartford Connection

Many New England Federalists considered England the world's best defense against the tyrant Napoleon, not America's enemy. In 1814, anti-war Yankees called a convention at Hartford, Connecticut, to discuss the possible secession of New England from the Union. However they ended up endorsing state nullification of federal laws and a constitutional amendment limiting executive and legislative power over foreign affairs.

B.   The Early Years of the War

The borderline disloyalty of New England was a big problem for James Madison, but he made many of his own problems. He chose William Hull and William Henry Harrison for his first generals; and both promptly lost territory to the British and their Indian allies. The New York militia refused to fight at the Niagara River; the only American victories in the first year were on the sea. Captain Oliver Perry got control of Lake Erie in the second year of the war. Tecumseh's confederation was also defeated in 1813. Andrew Jackson earned prominence as an Indian fighter in Tennessee, ending the power of the southwestern tribes in 1814.

C.   The Last Campaigns

Napoleon was defeated by the British and her continental allies in 1814. Freed to fight in America, British troops invaded Washington, D.C. They burned the Capitol, the presidential mansion and most of the city's public buildings. The redcoats were not stopped until they attempted to take Baltimore. Francis Scott Key wrote the "Star Spangled Banner" in commemorating its defense. Andrew Jackson soundly defeated a force of British regulars with a motley militia army in New Orleans.

D.   The Peace of Ghent

The Battle of New Orleans, which occurred in January of 1815, would not have been fought if communication was faster in that year. On December 24, 1814, American and British negotiators had concluded a peace at Ghent, Belgium. No mention was made of any of the issues that had started the conflict. However the British were prepared to reinforce their troops in New Orleans had Jackson lost the battle. Jackson's victory also had a positive psychological impact on Americans concerned with British aggression. While the War of 1812 made Republicans into Nationalists, it destroyed the credibility of the Federalists, the previous party of nationalism which opposed the war.

IV.   Conclusions: Between 1880 and the end of Madison's second term American political attitudes underwent a shift from dislike for central government to a new sense of nationalism. With Napoleon defeated, peace returned to Europe and Americans could turn to the exploitation of their human and natural resources with a new sense of unity and self-confidence.

Learning Objectives

After reading Chapter 8, you should be able to:

1. Explain the shift in the Republican political outlook from strict construction of the constitution and states rights to advocacy of active centralized nationalism.

2. Account for Thomas Jefferson's practical approach to executive decision making.

3. Describe the circumstances of the Louisiana Purchase.

4. Account for the war between England and the United States in 1812.

5. Compare the goals and attitudes of Americans who supported the war and those who opposed it.

6. Describe the course of the War of 1812 with special reference to the scarcity of American victories.

7. Explain the special significance of Jackson's victory in the Battle of New Orleans as it relates to American national feeling in 1815.

Identifications

Identify the following terms as you read the chapter; also note the significance of the term.

1.	Virginia Resolution of 1798	2.	midnight appointees
3.	John Marshall	4.	Marbury vs. Madison
5.	Louisiana Purchase	6.	Robert L. Livingston
7.	Toussaint L'Ouverture	8.	right of deposit
9.	Napoleon	10.	Meriwether Lewis & William Clark
11.	Embargo Act	12.	U.S.S. Chesapeake
13.	Non-intercourse Act	14.	James Madison
15.	War Hawks	16.	Hartford Convention
17.	"Star Spangled Banner"	18.	Battle of New Orleans
19.	Peace of Ghent	20.	Andrew Jackson

Focus Your Reading

Employ the terms you have identified above in answering the following questions:

1.   Was there any good reason for fighting the British in 1812? What were the events that led Americans to finally declare war.

2.   Discuss the events surrounding the case of <u>Marbury vs. Madison</u> and compare Marshall's decision with the Virginia Resolutions of 1798. Why could it be argued that the real winner in <u>Marbury vs. Madison</u> was John Marshall, not Madison or Marbury?

3.   Discuss the circumstances surrounding the Louisiana Purchase? What was Jefferson's chief concern regarding the purchase?

Questions

Multiple Choice

1.   Before he was president, James Madison took a position against all of the following except
   a.   Hamilton's scheme to fund war debt
   b.   strict construction of the Constitution
   c.   the central power of the new government
   d.   postal roads

2.   John Marshall in his decision in <u>Marbury vs. Madison</u> held that
   a.   Marbury's claim was denied
   b.   the Judiciary Act of 1801 was unconstitutional
   c.   the Supreme Court was the final judge of constitutionality
   d.   all of the above

3.   One reason the French gave up the Louisiana Territory was
   a.   the King was put back in power
   b.   they lost Haiti in a revolt of the black population
   c.   the British asked Napoleon to sell it to America
   d.   Jefferson gave them a deal they couldn't refuse

4.   One reason Aaron Burr got involved in the plot to detach the west from the United States and set up a new country was that
   a.   his reputation was damaged by his role in Hamilton's death
   b.   he knew that Wilkinson would never betray him to Jefferson
   c.   he refused to deal with the British minister in Washington
   d.   all of the above

5.   The <u>Essex</u> decision of 1805 declared that
   a.   all West Indian products were neutral goods
   b.   British goods would no longer be exported to America
   c.   American goods would no longer be shipped to England
   d.   it was illegal for Americans to ship West Indian produce out of American ports

6.	Jefferson believed that the best way to deal with the undeclared naval war of the British against the United States was to
	a.	send the American navy to Great Britain
	b.	seek help from Napoleon against the British
	c.	place an embargo on all exports from the United States
	d.	all of the above

7.	The chief architects of western Indian problems during the Republican administrations were
	a.	the British
	b.	Jefferson's appointees in the new territories
	c.	the French
	d.	Federalist officeholders from earlier years

8.	Ultimately the most significant effect of General Harrison's victory against the Shawnees at Tippecanoe was
	a.	the Indians finally gave up their resistance to white settlement
	b.	the boost the battle gave to Harrison's political career
	c.	the spread of hostility against the whites to the entire west
	d.	the Indians learned their lesson

9.	Which of the following political leaders was not a War Hawk?
	a.	Spencer Percival
	b.	Henry Clay
	c.	John C. Calhoun
	d.	Felix Grundy

10.	All of the following are reasons that the Americans went to war in 1812 except
	a.	an upsurge of nationalism
	b.	James Madison's eagerness to fight
	c.	impressment and confiscation of American ships
	d.	the prospect of continued submission to Britain

11.	In which region was antiwar sentiment the strongest between 1812 and 1814?
	a.	New England
	b.	New York and Pennsylvania
	c.	the West
	d.	the South

12.	Although it was fought after the peace treaty was signed, the Battle of New Orleans was an important victory because
	a.	it boosted the career of Andrew Jackson
	b.	it ended the possibility of a British Empire on the lower Mississippi
	c.	it helped to destroy the Federalist Party
	d.	all of the above

13.	The War Hawks were
	a.	bird enthusiasts
	b.	a group of Congressmen from the West and the South who advocated war with England
	c.	anti-Federalists
	d.	advocates of secession

Essay

1.   Discuss the reasons that the federal court system became the center of the party conflict between the Federalists and the Republicans. Compare political weapons used in the conflict with weapons used in similar contests today.

2.   List the steps by which Jefferson modified the government that he inherited in 1800. How did he change his own attitudes toward government as time went on? How do you explain these changes?

3.   Discuss the causes of the War of 1812. Which are the most crucial to the outbreak of hostilities: geographical factors, sectional factors, economic factors or offended national feelings?

4.   What were the results of the Hartford Connection and its implications for future regional disputes; why did it produce antagonism toward Federalists?

CHAPTER 9

The American Economic Miracle

What Made It Possible?

Summary and Outline

Summary: In 1833, Michael Chevalier noted that Pittsburg was the Birmingham of America, a dirty and busy industrial city, which illustrated the immense changes that were taking place in the United Stares. On the eve of the Civil War in 1860, America would be an economic giant second only to Great Britain in the world. How did this miracle come about?

Outline: I.   Factors of Production: Historians and economists disagree about the origins of economic growth: some believe that increases in output can be explained by investment factors of production--labor, resources, capital, skills and technology; others see consumption as the dynamic element in growth. Cultural developments may also be added to the equation to understand how the United States created its abundance.

A.   Resources

The United States was richly endowed with fertile land, timber for construction and fuel, as well as iron, copper, petroleum and coal for future industrial use. Many of these resources went unused until the late nineteenth century.

B.   Labor

Resources would have remained untapped without men and women who were willing to use them. There were 8.5 million people in America; the country's labor shortage before 1815 was barely offset by a high birthrate. The growth of the black labor force in the South was limited by the end of the slave trade in 1808. European immigration did not add materially to the labor force until conditions in Ireland, Germany and Scandinavia after 1840 bought a deluge of new citizens in their most productive years. The population grew to 11 million in 1860.

C.   Public Schools and Economic Growth

In the United States a literate and trained labor force, human capital, was created by the public education system. Schools were substandard until concerned citizens--labor leaders, philanthropists and others--followed the lead of Horace Mann in linking education to economic growth. The refurbished system that resulted taught values and skills; secondary schools and education for women lagged behind state-supported schools. Seminaries filled in the gap and trained women to teach in public schools. By 1860 only Denmark had a higher ratio of students to total population.

D.   Technology

Americans proved to be very inventive during the colonial period; new patent laws and the scarcity of labor added incentives for mechanical improvements after the Revolution. Oliver Evans built a water-powered flour mill in the 1780s; Eli Whitney introduced both machine-made nails and interchangeable parts in the 1790s. The first feasible steamboat was launched by Robert Fulton in 1807; and in 1844 Samuel F.B. Morse transmitted the first telegraph message between cities. Between 1802 and 1847 engineering courses were added to the formal curriculum of several northeastern colleges.

E.   Growing Markets

The growing population as it became more skillful was an addition to the supply side of American economic growth. But markets increased as the needs of young families and immigrants stimulated construction, so the new growth had its demand as well. With each passing year American industry expanded to meet the home market for practical and luxury goods.

F.   Capital

Capital is not just money, but as economists use the term, money invested in machines, buildings, railroads, mines, that is tools that produce other commodities. When invested capital is the basis for economic growth. The early United States relied on foreign sources for such investment, not only in loans but money brought by immigrants. Other sources were foreign trade, earned for the most part by food and fiber exports, and personal savings, invested either in financial institutions or in corporations, which provided the safety of limited liability after 1830.

G.   Banks and Banking

Commercial banks acted as money machines which advanced cash or credit to business people who wanted to embark on a new enterprise. Banks had to be careful of unreliable borrowers, speculation, and money lent out beyond cautious reserves. Since they kept only enough capital on hand to pay routine expenses and handle withdrawals, banks had to keep the good faith of their depositors. "Runs" or panics could lead to demands for immediate payments and suspension of business or bankruptcy. Bank notes issued by state-chartered banks might have similar problems if too many such notes were printed.

H.   Growth of the Banking System

Despite its drawbacks the commercial banking system added to the pool of investment capital before the Civil War. Hamilton's Bank of the United States acted as a central bank before its demise in 1811. The Second Bank of the United States was chartered with three times the capital in 1816. State banks prospered as well, but in the West "wildcat" banks issued paper money without gold backing, encouraging a boom-and-bust pattern in the economy.

I.   Government Actions

Many Americans opposed a strong governmental role in economic development, especially old-line Jeffersonians and followers of Adam Smith. The government's role in the country's growth was clear, however. Corporation laws enabled individuals to pool capital for new businesses, protective tariffs encouraged American industries, and the tax system rested easily on investors. Some states joined with investors to build railroads, canals. and wagon roads. Federal funds built the National Road, the St. Mary's Falls ship canal and many new harbors and lighthouses.

II. The Course of American Economic Growth: The United States was endowed by nature with resources and by immigration with a skilled population committed to hard work. How did these elements coalesce to produce an economic miracle?

A. The Birth of King Cotton

The major advance in American agriculture before the Civil War was the growth of King Cotton. India could not produce enough raw cotton to supply English mills; and the short-fiber cotton grown in the American South had seeds which were difficult to remove until Yankee inventor Eli Whitney invented his simple "gin" that could do the job easily. By the eve of the Civil War the southern United States had become the chief supplier of cotton to the world market.

B. The North and the West

Wheat was king in the North; bread was the staple food of the urban diet. Wheat-growing moved westward to the treeless prairies of the Midwest. Farm production increased as food prices went down, partly as a result of Hussey and McCormick's invention of horse-drawn reapers. By 1860, midwestern farmers were utilizing 80,000 harvesting machines, more than all other countries combined.

C. Land Policy

The comparatively large size of the American farm was the product of a deliberate government policy to provide family farms at low cost. The Land Act of 1804 lowered the price to $1.64 an acre and required a minimum purchase of 160 acres. Western land speculation played a part in financial panics in 1819 and 1837. Squatters benefited from several land laws which assisted those who farmed the public domain. Southern slaves owners and employers blocked a homestead act until 1862.

D. Steamboats and Roads

Two transportation resources that would not be fully utilized until canals and steamboats were developed were the Great Lakes and the Mississippi River. The Fulton group attempted to monopolize river traffic until its privileges were removed by the Supreme Court decision to open navigation to all investors in Gibbons vs. Ogden. State and federal funds were then spent to deepen channels, construct canals around obstructions and build lighthouses on the Great Lakes. Private turnpikes were supplemented by state and federal investment in all-weather roads.

E. Canals

The canal boom stated with the construction of the Erie Canal between 1817 and 1825; it connected the Great Lakes with the Atlantic Ocean, utilizing 83 locks, stone aqueducts and 363 miles of ditch between Lake Erie and the Hudson River. The canal lowered freight rates between New York and Buffalo and earned enough revenue to build new canals. By 1840 there were 3,300 miles of man-made waterways connecting the manufacturers of the East with their customers in the West.

F.   The Railroads Arrive

Railroads were especially welcomed by eastern merchants who were in competition with New York City. Rail technology improved gradually with the introduction of all-iron rails, locomotive cowcatchers, dependable boilers and swiveling wheels. All-weather routes were built where canals and rivers did not go. By 1860, the country had 30,000 miles of track.

G.   The Factory System

The future course of American economic growth was most significantly chartered by the expansion of the New England textile industry. Samuel Slater's cotton-spinning plant in Providence, Rhode Island, was the first such mill; but Francis Cabot Lowell's Boston Manufacturing Company at Waltham, Massachusetts, was a bigger success. Young women were hired to work at Lowell's new mill on the Merrimack River, lured by promises of good wages, dormitory housing and moral education. The women prospered until the 1840s when economic conditions brought lower wages and replacement by Irish immigrant workers.

III.   Industrial Workers: Americans were wealthy by the standards of the early nineteenth century.

A.   Unequal Gains

The gross national product doubled between the mid-1830s and the Civil War. The urban class benefited most from this burst of economic growth; others who gained were factory operatives, engineers, clerks, bookkeepers and managers. White-collar employees earned higher incomes and had more social standing than blue-collar workers in the new industries. "New men" in manufacturing and land holding built large fortunes at everyone else's expense.

B.   Wages and Working Conditions

Taken as a whole, American workers advanced in wage-earning capacity in the decade before the Civil War. Wages for working people in 1850 ranged from one dollar a week for domestic service to as much as $30 a week for a skilled iron worker. A family of five in New York City needed about $10 a week. While they were better off than their European counterparts, the lives of American workers were not easy. The Lowell girls worked twelve hours a day, six days a week. Work accidents were common and injuries usually meant lost income. Periodic depressions brought hardship to all workers. Charities were few in number and public assistance consisted of poor houses or asylums for paupers. Many skilled workers such as shoemakers saw their work downgraded by the introduction of power machinery and ready-made products turned out by low-paid operatives.

C.   The Labor Movement

Declining wages brought the first "turn-outs" to the idyllic factory system at Lowell. Most strikes before the Civil War were unplanned uprisings in which workers responded to abrupt changes such as wage cuts . However long-standing grievances produced the first city-wide labor unions, which were able to organize national unions by the 1830s. All but a few of these groups were destroyed by the Panic of 1837. The work ethic was very strong in the first half of the nineteenth century, and on the whole the American work force participated enthusiastically in the upsurge that made the pre-Civil War economic miracle possible.

IV. **Conclusions:** The economic growth of ante-bellum America was a product of abundant resources, a hard-working skillful population of native-born and immigrant citizens, foreign investment, direct government investment in canals and roads, entrepreneurship, low wages and low taxes, and the work ethic which was instilled by the schools and churches.

Learning Objectives

After reading Chapter 9, you should be able to:

1. List the factors that were responsible for the increase in American economic output that characterized the first half of the nineteenth century.

2. Describe the role of education in economic growth.

3. List significant advances in technology from 1790 to improvement and industrial development.

4. Describe the interaction between foreign investment and domestic capital in the financial foundation of growth.

5. Explain the role of government in economic growth.

6. Describe the improvements in transportation between 1807 and 1860.

7. Account for inequities in wealth in ante-bellum America.

8. Recount the role of government land policy in distribution of farmland and regional differences in agricultural products.

9. Describe the development of the factory system.

10. Analyze the early development of labor unions and their demise before the Civil War.

Identifications

Identify the following terms as you read the chapter; also note the significance of the term.

1. iron belt   2. Horace Mann

3. cult of domesticity   4. Eli Whitney

5. Clermont   6. limited liability

7.	Second Bank of the United States	8.	National Roads
9.	King Cotton	10.	Cyrus McCormick
11.	Gibbons vs. Ogden	12.	Baltimore and Ohio
13.	Francis Cabot Lowell	14.	Gibbons vs. Ogden
15.	Panic of 1837		

Focus Your Reading

Employ the terms you have identified above in answering the following questions:

1. How was the re-definition of the home in the cult of domesticity related to the development of a factory system and its corresponding refinement of the idea of work?

2. An important point made by the author concerns the level of education necessary to sustain economic growth in a modern society.

3. What is the argument between those who oppose a governmental role in business and economic development and those who favor it?

4. Discuss the impact of technology in the nineteenth century and the roles played by Whitney, Lowell, McCormick and railroads.

Questions

Multiple Choice

1. All of the following are factors of production essential to economic growth except
   a. technology
   b. economic advisors
   c. skills
   d. capital

2. A trained labor force, that is, human capital, was created mainly by
   a. large farm families
   b. foreign investment
   c. the American public education system
   d. immigration

3. The "cult" of domesticity" was the idea that
   a. women were equal to men
   b. women in their own spheres were a wasted resource

    c.   women should be trained to be household servants
    d.   women were inferior to men

4.   Which principle allowed corporation charters to become the main form of business organization by 1860?
    a.   limited liability
    b.   partnership
    c.   joint stock companies
    d.   savings banks

5.   American national and state governments were involved in building all of the following except
    a.   turnpikes
    b.   canals
    c.   textile mills
    d.   railroads

6.   Which type of cotton could not be grown profitably until the introduction of the cotton gin?
    a.   Upland short fiber cotton
    b.   Sea Island cotton
    c.   Indian cotton
    d.   all of the above

7.   Gibbons vs. Ogden dealt with
    a.   monopoly control of inland waterways
    b.   the power of the courts to declare laws invalid
    c.   the charter of national banks
    d.   the sale of public lands

8.   Which of the following "facts" concerning the Erie Canal is not true?
    a.   it was proposed by Mayor De Witt Clinton of New York
    b.   it connected the Atlantic Ocean with the Great Lakes
    c.   it was a financial failure
    d.   it was built by engineers who improvised as they went

9.   Which areas of the United States lacked railroad mileage on the eve of the Civil War?
    a.   the Atlantic Coast
    b.   Missouri and the Midwest
    c.   New Orleans and the South
    d.   the Great Plains and the Pacific Coast

10.   Which of the following groups had the highest income in 1850?
    a.   the Lowell girls
    b.   common labors
    c.   blacksmiths
    d.   textile department superintendents

11.   The uncertainties of pre-Civil War employment included
    a.   unemployment
    b.   job-related injuries
    c.   bad weather
    d.   all of the above

12. An area of the country that was chronically short of mechanics and laborers was
    a. the West
    b. the Northwest
    c. the Midwest
    d. the South

Essay

1. How much capital came from inside the United States and how much came from foreign sources before the Civil War? Does it matter one way or another? How ?

2. Discuss the role of technology and invention in development of a market economy.

CHAPTER 10

Jacksonian Democracy

What Was It and How Did It Change Political Life?

Summary and Outline

Summary: When Andrew Jackson was finally elected president of the United States in 1828, rough-looking men with defiant attitudes poured into Washington, frightening its long-time residents into reluctant flight. Was this a revolution which brought the common man to power? What kind of change did Jacksonian democracy bring about?

Outline: I. **The Era of Good Feelings:** The Federalists were no longer a factor in the politics of the "Era of Good Feelings." Most Federalist policies were incorporated into the Republican program: a new Bank of the United States, a protective tariff, and a bill to fund major internal improvements. Political opposition was limited to intraparty struggles among sectional political leaders. The presidents succeeded one another in a cut-and-dried process that discouraged many voters.

A.   The Virginia Dynasty

The presidents who served from Jefferson to Monroe (1800-1825) all came from Virginia. John Quincy Adams of Massachusetts succeeded Monroe; he was a gifted leader who supported science, the arts and economic progress. But like the Virginians he was aloof and humorless; in spite of his bold outlook and intelligence, Adams made little impression on Congress or the voters.

B.   John Marshall's Court

Supreme Court Chief Justice John Marshall was the only effective leader of the Era of Good Feelings. In 1810 in Fletcher vs. Peck, he struck down a state law for the first time. In the Dartmouth College Case he upheld the sanctity of contracts. In McCulloch vs. Maryland, he decided that the Second Bank of the United States could be taxed by Congress, but not by states.

C.   Foreign Affairs

Although they broke no new ground in domestic affairs, the Virginians and Adams were successful champions of American foreign interests. Florida was acquired from Spain by Adams in 1819 after Andrew Jackson's border raids convinced Spain that Florida was lost. When Spain also lost its colonies in America to revolution, Great Britain decided that cooperation with the United States was in order. This resulted in an agreement between Secretary of State Adams and British Foreign Secretary George Canning in 1823 that came to be known as the Monroe Doctrine.. It stated that the European monarchies were no longer welcome in American affairs.

D.   Missouri Compromise

When Missouri asked to be admitted as a slave state in 1819, Representative James Tallmadge of New York offered an amendment to the statehood bill which not only limited the growth of slavery in the new state but also provided for gradual emancipation of slave children. After heated debate, Congress decided to admit two new states to the Union: Missouri as a slave state and Maine, carved out of Massachusetts, as a new free state. For the rest of the territory of the Louisiana Purchase the dividing line between slave and free states was set at the southern boundary of Missouri (36° 30" north latitude)

II.   Jackson Rises to Power: John Quincy Adams was Monroe's logical successor based on the system utilized by the Virginia dynasty. However in 1824 Americans were less willing to accept decisions made at the top no matter how decent and learned the man chosen might be.

A.   Democratic Reforms in the States

The last vestiges of property qualifications were eliminated in the seaboard states, as some leaders warned colleagues that young voters would be attracted to open land in the western states. Printed ballots replaced "stand up" voting, and state legislatures were reapportioned more fairly. Appointive offices became elective, and conventions replaced caucuses in the nominating process. The eastern states became pioneers in democratic reforms, most of which preceded Andrew Jackson's rise to power.

B.   The Election of 1824

The Republican party nomination of 1824 was a popularity contest. J.Q. Adams got the official party recommendation, but he was opposed by Andrew Jackson, William Crawford of Georgia and Henry Clay of Kentucky. Jackson won the popular vote and was the leading vote getter in the electoral college. However no one candidate got a majority so the House of Representatives had to choose who would be president. Henry Clay threw his support to Adams and was later appointed Secretary of State. Jackson's supporters charged that a "corrupt bargain" had been struck to deny their hero the presidency. An atmosphere of hostility between Congress and President Adams resulted from the charge.

C.   The Tariff of Abominations

Adams and Jackson fought one another throughout Adams' administration. The protective tariff provided the main issue that separated them. Senator Martin Van Buren of New York wanted to increase Jackson's chances in 1828 by proposing a new tariff that would gain support for Jackson in the North and West. However as a result of compromises made during congressional debate, a bill emerged that no one supported. John C. Calhoun was so outraged that he published an Exposition and Protest against the tariff, claiming that offended states in the South could declare it null and void.

D.   The Election of 1828

Personal issues and mudslinging dominated the election of 1828. In the first major party convention the National Republicans renominated John Quincy Adams. Andrew Jackson, with John C. Calhoun as his running mate, was nominated by Tennessee. Both candidates were accused of horrendous crimes and moral lapses. No one knew Jackson's position on the tariff and internal improvements. Adams was generally supported by New Englanders and former Federalists, Jackson by southerners and western farmers. Jackson won the contest decisively, both in the popular and electoral vote count.

III. <u>King Andrew</u>

A. The Spoils System

Jackson wanted to reward his followers when he assumed office, but he did not remove former officeholders in a wholesale manner. Past historians tended to treat Jackson's "spoils system" as a democratization of the political process; yet Old Hickory's appointees had about the same social background as the people they replaced.
The new system was an incentive for ambitious men to work for the party in power; but it was both less efficient and more open to corruption than the civil system before it. The Jackson party infused a more open spirit into political life, but lowered its moral tone.

B. Jackson's Style

Andrew Jackson was a former soldier who did not take kindly to defiance or obstructionism. He was neither learned nor a consistent thinker; and he acted on attitudes acquired as a youth and never abandoned. He was a slave holder, a southerner and an old Indian fighter. He inspired either intense hatred or affection as Jackson tended to personalize his political attitudes. While he regarded them as enemies, Jackson's opponents proudly identified themselves as <u>Whigs,</u> who opposed the absolution of "King Andrew."

C. The Nullification Crisis

Jackson did not plan to reduce tariff rates drastically even though southerners believed that his criticism of the Tariff of Abominations put the president on their side. Jackson approved the slightly lower rates passed by Congress in 1832; Vice President Calhoun replied by issuing the South Carolina Ordinance of Nullification, declaring the new tariff void in his home state. Nullification was actually an aggressive stance against northern anti-slavery attitudes. Jackson took it to be an attack on his presidency, and asked Congress for a Force Bill that would grant him new powers to enforce customs laws. Clay assisted Jackson in lowering the tariff with the passage of the Force Bill. South Carolina rescinded nullification when no support came from other states, and the crisis to the Union was over.

D. Indian Policy

Jackson could be a strong nationalist when it suited his political outlook; however he could be equally defiant when national policy was not in accord with his prejudices. He had coerced the Cherokees in Georgia to exchange their tribal lands for land in the West, with the provision that Indian families could remain if they became farmers. To Jackson's disgust most families stayed in Georgia and became slave-owning cotton planters. In other areas, President Monroe's policy of moving tribes piecemeal beyond the Mississippi was speeded up by bribery and military threats. The Cherokees would not move, however; and their suit to stay in Georgia was upheld by Chief Justice Marshall in <u>Worcester vs. Georgia</u>. President Jackson refused to enforce the decision, instead signing an Indian Removal Act which authorized the forcible removal of all eastern tribes. The Seminoles rebelled and the Cherokees resisted, but both were eventually forced to move. The Cherokees lost 4,000 people on the "Trail of Tears" to Oklahoma.

E. The Attack on the Bank

Jackson hated the Bank of the United States more than he hated the Indians. Like his western supporters the president disliked all banks and paper money. Though the bank supplied credit and lent balance to the economy, it inspired hostility as the nation's largest corporation. Its president, Nicholas Biddle, had tremendous financial influence. He applied for a renewal of the Bank charter in 1832, but Jackson vetoed the measure. Jackson's veto message was denounced by Daniel Webster and others in the employ of the Bank, while Jackson's supporters condemned Biddle's "monster" as a bastion of monopoly and privilege.

F.   Whigs and Democrats

Jackson's party, guided by Martin Van Buren, formed a coalition of low-tariff, hard money, antimonoply-minded voters who called themselves Democrats. Internal improvements were favored by many Jacksonians, however; and in New York and New England they backed banks and high tariffs. The opposition party, called Whigs, were solid in their support of tariffs, banks, and internal improvements. However the differences between the parties' ideologies and those who supported them were not sharp. The Whigs were strongest in New England; but they had support from large planters who needed credit in the South and western farmers who needed internal improvements. The new party nominated Henry Clay and the Democrats renominated Jackson, with Martin Van Buren as his new running mate, in 1832. Jackson won his second term in a decisive victory.

G.   Economic Ups and Downs

President Jackson interpreted his re-election as a mandate to uncharter the Second Bank of the United States. He removed government deposits from the institution and placed them in twenty-three state banks, labeled "pet banks" by the Whigs. Biddle was forced to call in his loans, contracting credit, while the pet banks indulged in wild land speculation. Jackson realized that his cure was worse than the Bank's original disease. He issued a Specie Circular in 1836 announcing that the federal government would accept only hard money for land sales. State bank notes took a nose dive, land sales plummeted and severe panic ensued that halted business expansion after 1837.

IV.   **Politics After Jackson:**

A.   The Van Buren Administration

Martin Van Buren of New York was the heir to Jackson; and he won a comfortable victory in 1836 because the Whigs failed to mount an effective national campaign against him. When the economic storm accompanying the Panic of 1837 broke, Van Buren responded timidly, citing a solid if lately embraced philosophy of "laissez faire" government. The Democrats did manage to establish an Independent Treasury System which did not rely on private banks, but its transactions were confined to hard money collections and payments.

B.   The Whigs Take Power

Despite his record of timid actions in the face of hard times, Van Buren received no serious challenge to his bid for renomination in 1840. The Whigs turned to an old military hero untarnished by past political commitments, William Henry Harrison. He was advised to avoid saying anything about his political views; and when he seemed to be insulted by the Democratic claim that Harrison should retire to a log cabin with a barrel of hard cider, the aristocratic image of the Whig candidate was removed. A campaign ensued which was mostly ballyhoo, parades and cider parties. The Whigs claimed that Van Buren was the aristocrat who lived on his large estate, while "Tippecanoe" Harrison was the simple patriot who lived in a log cabin. The Whigs received 53 per cent of the popular vote and turned out the incumbent Van Buren.

V.   Conclusions: Jackson's election in 1828 did not revolutionize the social and political order of the United States, but it did result in a new political framework. A revitalization of American political life followed Jackson's tenure in office which brought the country both a strong two-party system and a government which was more responsive to public wants and needs. Both parties now had to accept or appear to accept the concept of a sovereign people.

Learning Objectives

After reading Chapter 10, you should be able to:

1.   Assess the contributions of the Virginia Dynasty and the Supreme Court to political stability before 1824.

2.   Understand the role of John Quincy Adams in American foreign policy statements and the settlement of boundary disputes.

3.   Describe the democratization process before the Civil War both before and after the Jacksonian presidency.

4.   Compare the campaigns and outcomes of the elections of 1824 and 1828.

5.   Explain the political and personal hostility that developed between Jackson and Calhoun.

6.   Understand the origin and course of the nullification controversy.

7.   Account for Jackson's Indian policy.

8.   Analyze Jackson's war on the Bank of the United States.

9.   Explain the emergence of the second two-party system.

10.   Assess the immediate and long-term impact of Jacksonian Democracy.

Identifications

Identify the following terms as you read the chapter, also note the significance of the term.

1.   Old Hickory   2.   John Quincy Adams

3.   Fletcher vs. Peck   4.   Adams-Onis Treaty

5.   Monroe Doctrine   6.   Missouri Compromise

7.	corrupt bargain	8.	John C. Calhoun
9.	Martin Van Buren	10.	<u>Exposition and Protest</u>
11.	Whigs	12.	Ordinance of Nullification
13.	*Worcester vs. Georgia*	14.	Indian Removal Act
15.	Trail of Tears	16.	Nicholas Biddle

Focus Your Reading

Employ the terms you have identified above in answering the following questions:

1. Analyze Chief Justice Marshall's position as it develops in the important cases decided by the Supreme court between 1810 and 1840. Using the court cases listed above, discuss how Marshall created and defined judicial authority.

2. What was Jackson's Indian Policy, the case of <u>Worcester vs. Georgia</u>, and the long term effect of removal?

3. Discuss the events and political arguments on both sides surrounding the tariffs of 1820 and 1830, the Exposition and Protest and the nullification crisis. What were the underlying southern concerns? What were the implications of the crisis?

4. What is the proof that the Whigs learned their political lessons from the Jacksonians in 1840? What has been the long-term impact of the "Log Cabin and Hard Cider" campaign on all political campaigns since 1840?

Questions

Multiple Choice

1. All of the following were qualities that made Andrew Jackson a popular leader except
    a. bluntness
    b. intelligence and learning
    c. courtliness and charm
    d. military leadership

2. The Supreme Court decisions in Fletcher vs. Peck and the Dartmouth College Case both dealt with
    a. the validity of contracts
    b. the ability of a state to tax federal money issues
    c. the appointment of judges
    d. the right to review state court decisions

3. All of the following were original principles in the Monroe Doctrine except
   a. no future European colonization in the Americas
   b. all American nations would remain republican
   c. the United States would stay out of European affairs and respect existing European colonies
   d. the United States reserved the right to remove offensive American governments

4. In most cases the first states to remove property qualifications for voting were
   a. northeastern states
   b. southern states
   c. western states
   d. all of the above

5. Calhoun's anonymously written Exposition and Protest asserted all of the following points except
   a. Congress had no right to levy tariffs so high they would exclude imports
   b. the constitution meant tariffs to be revenue taxes only
   c. states could declare laws they considered unconstitutional to be null and void
   d. states had a right to leave the Union

6. In the election campaign of 1828, charges made by the partisans of one candidate against the other included
   a. the claim that Adams' wife was born out of wedlock
   b. the charge that Rachel Jackson was not divorced from her previous husband
   c. the claim that Jackson had killed six innocent soldiers
   d. all of the above

7. After Jackson's election to the presidency the main criterion for hiring and firing civil servants was
   a. loyalty to the president
   b. proven competence on the job
   c. merit examinations
   d. all of the above

8. All of the following were factors in the publication of the South Carolina Ordinance of Nullification except
   a. the abolition crusade of William Lloyd Garrison
   b. Jackson's refusal to lower tariff rates in 1832
   c. a drop in world cotton prices
   d. a frightened planter elite

9. The Indian tribe with the most to lose as a result of Jackson's removal policy was the
   a. Cherokee
   b. Chippewa
   c. Delaware
   d. Osage

10. The Log Cabin and Hard Cider campaign worked in favor of the Whigs in 1840 because
    a. Van Buren failed to alleviate the economic slump following the Panic of 1837

b.   Harrison was made to seem a common man and Van Buren the aristocrat
c.   Harrison had no known political principle
d.   all of the above

11.   Jackson opposed the Second National Bank because
a.   it put public money under the control of private individuals
b.   it was not subject to private control
c.   he had lost money to banks earlier and distrusted Eastern bankers
d.   all of the above

Essay

1.   Compare the achievements of the Jacksonians with the Virginia Dynasty. Which group was most responsible for America's economic upsurge? Which group had the better political leaders? Which group achieved more in foreign affairs? Be sure to list your criteria for judgment.

2.   Discuss Andrew Jackson's background. Which experiences prepared him for his presidency? Which were drawbacks? Did Jackson have a consistent philosophy?

3.   Was the Second Bank of the United States a positive or negative influence on the American economy in the 1820s and 1830s? What personal prejudices on the part of Jackson and Biddle got in the way in the Bank fight? What were the results?

4.   Discuss the life of Peggy Eaton (Timberlake Buchignani) as a Jacksonian "celebrity." Why did Jackson feel such affection for her? What was her role in the alienation of Jackson and Calhoun?

5.   Discuss the development of the Whig party and the "second two-party system." What groups supported each party?

Map Exercises

Locate or draw in the following and explain their significance.

North America circa 1830

1.   Land claimed by Spain

2.   Louisiana

3.   Missouri

4.   36' 30" parallel

5.   Land jointly claimed by Britain and the United States

6.   Illinois

7.   Virginia

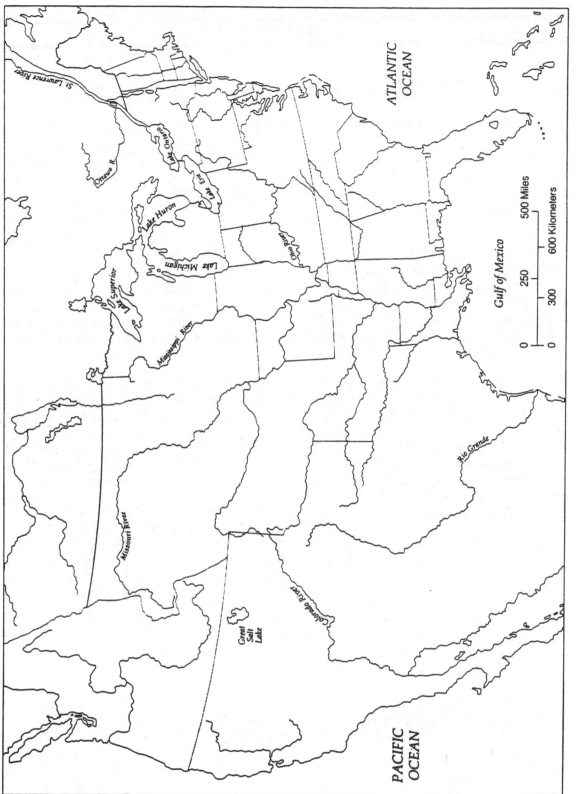

St. Lawrence River

Ottawa R.

Lake Ontario

Lake Erie

Lake Huron

Lake Superior

Lake Michigan

Mississippi River

Ohio River

Missouri River

Great Salt Lake

Colorado River

Rio Grande

ATLANTIC OCEAN

PACIFIC OCEAN

Gulf of Mexico

| 0 | 250 | 500 Miles |
| 0 | 300 | 600 Kilometers |

Map 8

CHAPTER 11

The Mexican War and Expansionism

Greed, Manifest Destiny or Inevitability?

Summary and Outline

Summary: Congress voted to go to war with Mexico on May 11, 1846, in response to President James K. Polk's solemn claim that American blood had been shed on American soil. However many Americans in and out of Congress were uneasy about the war. Abraham Lincoln of Illinois demanded that the President prove his allegation. New Englanders claimed that Polk wanted more land for slavery, and some historians have agreed with them. Others assert that the American occupation of Mexican territory was an inevitable consequence of Manifest Destiny. Which was it: imperialism and greed for land, or the working out of geopolitical law?

Outline: I.   The Oregon Country: Beyond the western boundary of the Louisiana Purchase lay a vast mountainous region barely touched by European culture. Title to the Oregon country was in dispute; the British claim was based on the voyages of Cook and Vancouver and the activities of fur-trading companies; the American claim was based on Captain Robert Gray's discovery of the Columbia River and the explorations of Lewis and Clark. Oregon was inhabited by salmon-fishing, woodworking Indian tribes along the coast and plateau fisherfolk and hunters and gathers in the interior.

A.   The Far Western Fur Trade

The dispute over Oregon was ultimately resolved when the United States sent the most settlers. The fur trade attracted the earliest European settlers. In 1811, John Jacob Astor established Astoria at the mouth of the Columbia; the American North West Company and the British Hudson's Bay Company entered Oregon and merged under British control in 1821. A Missourian named William Ashley sent out his own agents to find furs in 1825. His successors formed the Rocky Mountain Fur Company, which depended upon the work of wild-living "mountain men."

B.   The Way West

Agents of the fur companies opened up in the trans-Missouri region by marking routes, exploring rivers and finding new passes. Some explorers such as Zebulon Pike and Stephen Long doubted that the land was fit for cultivation. Long's account of a "Great American Desert" delayed settlement of the High Plains and Great Basin for several decades. Many American were deflected to Oregon, especially the Willamette Valley, by traveling the Oregon Trail in wagon trains. It was rough going until the emigrants arrived at the Dalles and floated westward down the Columbia River. Eventually the British Hudson River Company bowed to the inevitable and surrendered Oregon to the Americans; by 1845 the British conceded the entire area from Puget Sound to the California border.

84

II. **The Mexican Borderland:** Before Oregon was settled some Americans had been attracted to the dry Southwest, a million square miles of arid Mexican territory which included well-watered tracts in east Texas and the Central Valley of California.

A. The Native Peoples

There were few European settlers in the Mexican Southwest. Texas was populated by migratory Indian groups who hunted buffalo, adopting horses from the Spanish in the seventeenth century. Pueblo Indians lived in New Mexico and Arizona, grouped in agricultural communities arranged around central plazas. California tribes had simple economies and few material possessions; they passed down a rich heritage of myths and songs to later generations.

B. Spanish Penetration

The earliest Spanish settlers came to the Southwest after 1600 when Santa Fe, New Mexico, was founded. Missionaries came ahead of soldiers, establishing a pattern for frontier settlements. Vineyards, cultivated fields, herds of cattle and Indian huts surrounded mission churches in new communities organized by friars.

C. California

In 1769, Junipero Serra led a party of soldiers, friars and Indians from Arizona to San Diego Bay, establishing the first of twenty-one missions and two presidios which were sponsored by Spain to forestall Russian expansion in what is now California. The Franciscans hoped to Christianize the Indians, but a demographic disaster was the result. Large ranches were set up in the 1830s by the Mexican government; at the same time Americans also began drifting in as merchants and ranchers. Most Californians did not live the idyllic life of the ranchers.

D. New Mexico

The New Mexico Territory was separated from other Mexican borderlands by rugged plains and mountains. The Pueblo Indians had no need for the friars; while Comanches, Apaches and Navajos were so warlike they repelled the Europeans. They were not defeated until the mid-nineteenth century. The Spaniards set up a permanent settlement near Santa Fe; but it was not well supplied with goods until William Beckwell, a merchant from St. Louis, set up a lucrative trade with settlers in the 1820s.

E. Texas

Texas was the object of American settlement early in the nineteenth century. Stephen Austin was granted the right to set up a permanent settlement for 300 families in 1823 by the Mexican government. In exchange for conversion to Roman Catholicism each family got 4,000 acres. Although no more Americans were permitted to emigrate by law, by 1835 there were 30,000 living in Texas.

III. **The Annexation of Texas:** The Texas Revolution: Most Americans in Texas were not easily converted to Roman Catholicism nor were they pleased with Mexico's laws against slavery. However the Austin community remained loyal to the government to the south. The United States raised the pressure on Mexico in the 1830s by offering $5 million for Texas. At the same time Mexican governments proved to be inconsistent in their treatment of the province. Originally a federalist who believed in local autonomy for Mexican provinces, Antonio Lopez de Santa Anna became a centralist, and in

1834, he rescinded the self-rule granted to the Austin colony. When Santa Anna sent an army against them in 1836, fifty-nine delegates declared Texas to be independent and selected Sam Houston as their president. After defeats at the Alamo in San Antonio and Goliad, Houston stopped the Mexican army at San Jacinto. Santa Anna was obliged to grant Texas its independence with its southern boundary at the Rio Grande.

IV. Expansionism

A. Advocates and Opponents

John Tyler became president in 1841 when William Henry Harrison died a month after his inauguration. Tyler was a former Democrat who opposed the program of the Whig party. He vetoed two tariff bills before he signed the Tariff of 1842. In foreign affairs Tyler pursued a moderately expansionist course where slave territory was concerned. In the North, where a boundary dispute with Great Britain caused a great deal of trouble for Maine, Tyler remained aloof. Daniel Webster settled the Maine boundary; but in Oregon Tyler's indecision prevented a boundary agreement.

B. Victory for Tyler

Tyler achieved a diplomatic success in Texas. Many in the Whig party opposed annexation, while northern Democrats feared the expansion of slavery into Texas. Annexation, it was argued, could goad the Mexicans into war. Texans briefly negotiated with Great Britain to force Congress to support Tyler. It was all to little avail however until Tyler could use the election of a pro-annexation Democrat, James K. Polk, to ask Congress to approve a joint resolution to admit Texas to the Union in 1845.

V. Moving Toward War: James K. Polk, a late ballot "dark horse" at the Democratic convention in 1848, was not an impressive-looking man. The Mexican ambassador, who resigned when Texas was annexed to the United States, told his superiors that Polk's government had no stomach for war. But Polk could not be measured by his outward demeanor. He was a strong-willed man who was determined to make an impression. Mexico was his objective.

A. Manifest Destiny

First identified by John L. O'Sullivan, Manifest Destiny was the doctrine that the American people had the God-given right to spread their institutions from the Atlantic to the Pacific Coast. It was a self-serving ideology similar to nationalist ideals pursued by many nineteenth-century powers. The United States never pursued colonies, especially when large groups of diverse peoples were involved. However, President Polk never swerved in his determination to get all of Oregon, Texas to the Rio Grande and California.

B. Debate on Expansionism

Anti expansionism tended to be connected to antislavery sentiments. Southerners wanted Texas; commercial and industrial men in the Northeast wanted Pacific ports; people in the upper Mississippi wanted land in the Far West. Whigs believed that expansion was unethical, while many Democrats considered it an irrelevant issue. "Young America" Democrats led the movement for an all-American continent. President Polk was temperamentally a member of this group.

C.   Compromise with England

President Polk used the 54°40' demand on the Oregon—Washington border to bring the English around to a negotiating stance on the lower and more logical forty-ninth parallel. Secretary of State Buchanan accepted it in 1846. In the meantime, Americans and Mexicans were firing at one another along the southern border.

D.   The Slidell Mission

Polk was reluctant to go to war; so he sent John Slidell to Mexico City to negotiate the Rio Grande boundary for Texas. If possible he was to negotiate the sale of New Mexico and California as well. Patriots in Mexico were so upset by Slidell's mission that they insisted that the Herrera government ignore him. A new government began to negotiate with the British and gave Slidell his walking papers. By the spring of 1846, Polk believed that war with Mexico was inevitable, and ordered Zachary Taylor to move his troops to the disputed north bank of the Rio Grande. War was declared by a vote of 40 to 2 in the Senate and 174 to 14 in the House two days after Polk's war message was read to Congress.

VI.   War With Mexico: The Mexican War lasted for two years, cost 13,000 American lives and $100 million. Young men flocked to army recruiting offices to be led into conflict by well-trained West Pointers. Many Whigs remained skeptical of the war and antislavery people opposed it. However, most Americans supported the war and cheered its troops on to victory.

A.   Taking the Borderland

The Mexican War was fought on a wide front. Kearny's Army of the West captured Santa Fe, New Mexico, and crossed the desert to San Diego, California; Taylor's army routed General Arista's troops and marched southward to Monterrey, Mexico. American settlers in California declared a Bear Flag Republic; Captain John C. Fremont took over as leader of the revolt and captured Monterey. Mexican forces held southern California until Commodore Stockton's forces could be combined with Kearny's Army of the West.

B.   Victory in Mexico

Antonio Lopez de Santa Anna entered the scene just as American forces took control of the borderlands. He was defeated by a force of American volunteers at Buena Vista; turning southward he met General Winfield Scott as the American forces advanced on Mexico City. Santa Anna requested an armistice, but peace negotiations broke down. Scott took Mexico City after fierce fighting on September 13, 1847. Santa Anna fled the country and the war ended.

C.   The Peace

With Santa Anna gone, peace negotiator Nicholas Trist could find no one to talk to; Americans at first had moderate demands on Mexican territory; New Mexico and California. But as fervor over the war grew, "All Mexico" became the cry. There was talk of building a canal across the isthmus of Tehuantepec; but unsettled conditions in the newly captured Southwest convinced most Americans that the All Mexico idea was unwarranted. The Treaty of Guadalupe Hidalgo was finally signed on February 2, 1848, confirming the Rio Grande as the southern border of Texas and ceding the province of New Mexico and California to the United States. In return the United States paid Mexico $15 million and forgave $3.5 million in American claims.

Learning Objectives

After reading Chapter 11, you should be able to:

1.   Explain why the United States could not establish a clear claim to Oregon before 1846.

2.   Describe the Indian and Spanish settlement of the Mexican borderlands.

3.   Describe the American migration into California, New Mexico and Texas.

4.   Explain how Texas was annexed to the United States.

5.   Account for John Tyler's attitudes regarding Congress, his own party and expansionism.

6.   Analyze the drift of America and Mexico toward war.

7.   Describe Polk's attitude toward expansionism, war with Mexico and annexation of the borderlands.

8.   Compare the expansionist and anti-expansionist positions in regard to Mexican territory.

9.   Describe the circumstance, the progress and the results of the Mexican War.

Identifications

Identify the following terms as you read the chapter;also note the significance of the term.

1.	Manifest Destiny	2.	Adams-Onis Treaty
3.	Great American Desert	4.	Stephen Long
5.	Pueblo Indians	6.	Junipero Serra
7.	Vaqueros	8.	Stephen F. Austin
9.	Antonio Lopez de Santa Anna	10.	Sam Houston
11.	Alamo	12.	San Jacinto
13.	Webster Ashburton Treaty	14.	Oregon Trail
15.	General Zachary Taylor	16.	General Winfield Scott
17.	Treaty of Guadalupe Hidalgo		

Focus Your Reading

Employ the terms you have identified above in answering the following questions:

1. Compare the reactions of various tribes in the southwest to both Spanish and American settlement.

2. Discuss the settlement of Texas by Americans and the move toward independence.

3. What did the war with Mexico produce for the United States?

4. Discuss Manifest Destiny as a permanent attitude in American political life. How was it a factor in the early colonies and how did it influence Americans in Texas and Oregon?

5. Explain the process of expansion and settlement into the southwest of California and Mexico.

Questions

1. All of the following are interpretations of the causes of the Mexican War except
   a. the idea that the cotton South needed more territory
   b. the idea that war was the inevitable result of American cultural superiority
   c. the idea that it was caused by a small border incident
   d. the idea that the war arose out of the circumstances of history and geography

2. The British claim to Oregon was based on
   a. exploratory voyages and fur-trapping activities
   b. the discovery of the Columbia River
   c. the support of the woodworking and salmon-fishing Indians
   d. all of the above

3. Which of the following changes for women occurred on the Oregon Trail?
   a. pioneer society lacked gender distinctions
   b. women were found to be essential to survival in frontier society
   c. women had to learn to hunt and use weapons
   d. all of the above

4. Which of the following borderland tribes lives in agricultural communities consisting of structures that resembled modern apartment houses?
   a. Comanche Indians
   b. Apaches
   c. Pueblo Indians
   d. California Indians

5. Which of the following did the Pueblo Indians desire to acquire from the Spaniards?
   a. Christianity
   b. sheep, goats, and horses
   c. new methods of agriculture
   d. all of the above

6. Which of the following difficulties separated the Texans from their Mexican governors?
   a. religious differences
   b. attitudes of cultural superiority
   c. the desire to grow cotton with slave labor
   d. all of the above

7. Which of the following facts was most important in President Tyler's lack of influence with Congress?
   a. elected as a Whig, he still acted like a Democrat
   b. he was a blunt-speaking war hero
   c. he was a nationalist
   d. all of the above

8. Even though its popularity peaked during the years of the war with Mexico, Manifest Destiny could be traced as far back as
   a. the Puritans of Massachusetts Bay
   b. the Northwest Ordinance
   c. the Revolutionary War
   d. Columbus

9. "Fifty-four forty or fight" referred to
   a. the Rio Grande
   b. the area between the Nueces River and the Rio Grande
   c. the boundary between the Oregon Country and British Canada
   d. the Aroostook War in Maine

10. The war with Mexico was
    a. popular and costly
    b. unpopular and costly
    c. long and unpopular
    d. relatively short and inexpensive

11. The Treaty of Guadalupe Hidalgo provided for
    a. the annexation of California and New Mexico by the United States
    b. the payment of $15 million to Mexico
    c. the Rio Grande as the southern border of Texas
    d. all of the above

Essay

1. Discuss the origins of the Mexican War. Was it inevitable or could it have been prevented by careful diplomacy? What were its long-term results?

2. Explain the role of Manifest Destiny in the continental expansion of the United States.

3.	Discuss the reasons why most Americans wanted to annex California. What economic considerations were present?

4.	Discuss and trace the political developments and leaders who fostered an expansionist policy from 1840 to 1848. Who were the big players in the Oregon dispute and the Maine border dispute?

CHAPTER 12

Americans Before the Civil War

What Were They Really Like?

Summary and Outline

Summary: Most European writers found Americans to be very democratic, essentially unconcerned with status and gender. However some also noticed a fear of isolation and tendency to conform to public opinion. Americans could be money seekers, yet also charitable and respectful of books and learning. An examination of American culture, institutions and values which concentrates on the ante-bellum North and West can reconcile these seemingly conflicting views.

I. **The Moving Frontier:** Before 1860, the West was the fastest-growing part of the United States. Half of the 31 million people living in the nation on the eve of the Civil War were living west of the Appalachian Mountains. Americans moved westward along latitude lines, that is, from New England to Illinois, even Oregon, and from the South to Kentucky, Tennessee and the Gulf region. Most slaves moved west with their masters.

A.   The Migrant's Motives

People moved west because they were restless, that is, prone to change their residences even within cities. However some were refugees, people fleeing the law, creditors, spouses or mothers and fathers. Single women found the West to be a land of opportunity where they could meet young unmarried farmers. Cheap, fertile land proved to be the biggest draw in westward migration, especially for southerners whose cotton land in the Chesapeake region and the Carolinas suffered from soil exhaustion.

B.   The Frontier Type

Fredrick Jackson Turner's interpretation of the West has impressed many Americans in and out of the history profession: the rugged individualist with a Colt 45 was a central figure of national mythology. "Dudes" from the east seemed to need lessons in democracy; "posses" demonstrated the importance of cooperative action. Much of this was exaggerated, however: individualism was not unqualified, and many communities such as the Mormons moved West as one large group. While many westerners were self-reliant and tolerant, many others were lawless and given to drunkenness and swearing. Though they were generally egalitarian, westerners were always impressed by money.

II.   New Pressures in the Northeast: Turner viewed the West as the source of democratic values for the nation as a whole. This interpretation ignored the economic changes that turned New England farm people into factory wage earners and lured immigrants to America from Europe. Such changes were unrelated to the Western experience.

A.   Problems of Urbanization

For one thing Turner ignored urbanization. While there were only five cities with 10,000 inhabitants or more in 1800, by the eve of the Civil War there were over 100,000. Philadelphia had 500,000 and New York and Brooklyn together had one million. Such cities had the advantages of large metropolitan services, but they also suffered from social problems. Transportation and housing were two such problems; bad water supplies, poor waste disposal and inadequate health care workers were others. Typhoid fever and typhus were common; cholera was caused by infected water supplies in 1832 and 1850. Most of the large water systems exchanged polluted wells for aqueducts by mid-century.

B.   Crime and Violence

The general violence and disorder of pre-Civil War American life was magnified in the cities. City slums like New York's Five Points produced gangs that carried on full scale wars with the police. Immigrants were crowded into violence-prone districts, prompting native-born Americans to conclude that foreigners were criminals. The constable and "watch" system used in most cities was replaced by a full-time professional police force in New York City in the 1840s.

C.   Surging Immigration

Equality was an American ideal, but it was challenged by increasing tensions between native-born and more recently arrived citizens. The largest immigrant groups, the Irish and the Germans, did not fare equally well in America. Irish peasants came in the 1840s when the potato crop failed; they were forced to stay in the cities and take menial jobs. Germans came to the United States with money from selling land and a variety of craft skills. They moved from the cities to the rich farm lands of Illinois and Wisconsin, integrating easily into midwestern life.

D.   Discrimination

Americans often spoke of equality, but native-born citizens were not used to large blocks of aliens in their midst. Mostly Protestants, native-born people also reacted negatively to Roman Catholic immigrants with their highly centralized church. Anti-foreign feeling caused violent confrontations between Catholics and Protestants between 1830 and 1860; job discrimination against the Irish was common during hard times. The Know-Nothing Party entered politics in the 1850s with a "nativist" platform, but it split up because of the slavery issue.

E.   Free Blacks

Race was the biggest test of American equality. Free Blacks prospered in some specialty trades: sail making, barbering and as restauranteurs. But in most cases blacks were employed as laborers; they were also the object of bigotry, discrimination and Jim Crow laws. Blacks organized their own churches and lodges rather than accept inferior status in white organizations. Tensions between blacks and poor white immigrants sometimes erupted into full-scale riots.

F.   Women

Like all western societies, the United States was male-dominated in the early nineteenth century. Under the law women were treated as minors; their property belonged to their husbands. Women could not vote or hold office; the only profession that would admit them was school teaching. All "women's work" was poorly paid, unskilled or both. They worked with their husbands in family groups on the farms; but as the country became more urban, husbands increasingly went to work, leaving their wives and children at home. Women acquired a "sphere" in middle class homes, but they continued to be treated as fragile creatures who had to be protected from the world.

III.   Everday Life: Though Americans averaged the second highest per capita income in the world by 1860, most American lives were uncomfortable by our standards.

A.   Housing

Housing standards were poor, dirt and smells were unavoidable, personal hygiene was at a minimum.

B.   Changes

With economic prosperity daily lifestyles improved and diets became more diverse. Men (and women) used tobacco in large amounts.

IV.   The Arts in Ante-bellum America: Just as eqalitarian sentiments in America were limited by various prejudices; idealism was compromised by materialism. Yet in the nineteenth century Americans were also very creative in the arts, especially in painting, literature and architecture.

A.   An American Literature

Americans produced no distinctive literature before 1800. Then abruptly Washington Irving and James Fenimore Cooper were influenced by the ground swell of European romanticism. Romantics were interested in individual emotions, death, horror and crime. Washington Irving published several works set in the Hudson River Valley and the Catskill Mountains which emphasized legends of the area. More authentically than Irving, Cooper used the early frontier as a setting for novels that described the struggle to bring civilization to the wilderness. He started an American tradition of modest heroes when he created Natty Bumpo, an untutored frontiersman who struggled against the dangers of the forest, in the Leatherstocking Tales.

B.   The New England Renaissance

Edgar Allan Poe was very much an American writer in his fondness for mystery and violence; but he appears less consistent with what Americans wanted to be than the great writers of the New England Renaissance. Boston had a literary back ground based on the Puritan clergy; but its nineteenth-century stature was a product of transcendentalism, a distinctly New World blend of European romanticism and oriental mysticism. Its leading exponent was Ralph Waldo Emerson, a high-minded moralist who inspired the establishment of Brook Farm, a utopian cooperative community attended by most of the New England writers. Henry David Thoreau tried to live an even simpler existence at Walden Pond. Nathaniel Hawthorne did not share many of the Boston group's ideas; though he too rejected materialism, he was more interested in the capacity of men and women to do evil to one another. After publishing The Scarlet Letter, in 1850 and The House of the Seven Gables, in 1851, he satirized the Brook Farm experiment in The Blithedale Romance, published in 1852.

C. Melville and Whitman

Another writer who was not a transcendentalist was Herman Melville, who wrote his masterpiece Moby Dick (1850), after publishing several South Seas adventure stories. Walt Whitman also moved against the trends of his age, combining arrogance with vigorous advocacy in Leaves of Grass (1855) and Democratic Vistas (1871).

D. The Fireside Poets

Four pre-Civil War narrative or patriotic poets were American favorites for many years. However anachronistic they appear now, Bryant, Holmes, Lowell and Longfellow validated the ideals and values of the literate citizens of an earlier era.

E. The People's Literature

The New England and New York writers were the first American intellectuals who rebelled against the values of their society. Popular writers, on the other hand, endorsed them heartily in inexpensive novels that poured out of the ante-bellum press. Blood and thunder thrillers, domestic novels that praised true love and household virtues, and melodramatic heroes and heroines were greedily embraced by the public.

F. Painting

Conventional academic painters were not successful in America; but those that chose the American countryside as the subjects of their work got public attention. Hudson River school painters, Thomas Cole and Asher Durand were idyllic and romantic, while George Catlin and John Audubon were less sentimental. Catlin's Indians and Audubon's birds were carefully drafted; they still attract scientific as well as aesthetic interest.

G. The Romantic and the Practical in Architecture

The main American innovation in architecture was the balloon-frame, which was the forerunner of the contemporary light skeleton of uprights and cross members attached by nails. For those who wanted more permanent quarters gracious mansions were still commissioned in the Greek revival style. Both Greek and Gothic styles were used for public buildings, but the Gothic style was most suited to private residences built to a romantic ideal in the past.

V. The Perfect Society:

American materialism and conformity were contradicted by a degree of dissent in ante-bellum society that has seldom been expressed since. The reform impulse of the period brought forth a confusion of voices and actions: people wanted to change the treatment of prisoners, the mentally ill, and the intemperate; they also wanted to end war, extend women's rights, abolish slavery and create ideal communities.

A. Religious Roots of Reform

One of the great swings in religious enthusiasm that characterized the response of Americans from the past to the present took place in the nineteenth century. During the so-called Second Great Awakening traveling bands of evangelists railed at Americans to reconsider their sins or reaffirm their faith at vast outdoor revivals. The converted, proclaimed the preacher Charles Finney, "should aim at being holy and not rest till they are perfect as God." This perfectionist ideal permeated all organizations involved in humanitarian efforts to improve society.

B.   The Desire for Control

Not all reformers were perfectionists; some believed that urban industrial society was in danger of collapse. The family was often blamed for its inability to discipline its members; asylums were recommended as havens from the harsh world. Penitentiaries were built to separate first offenders from hardened criminals and rehabilitate them. Asylums were also built for the mentally ill. Alcoholism was a concern of both religious and social reformers. The former warned about working-class drinking and lewd behavior, while the latter joined temperance movements to persuade state legislatures to prohibit the production and sale of alcoholic beverages.

C.   Growing Female Assertiveness

At one time the large number of women in the nineteenth-century reform movement was ascribed to the "nurturing qualities" of women. However it seems obvious these days that young women who were educated in the seminaries found the social setting of their day very confining. It was also more acceptable to strive for the rights of others rather than women's rights. Middle-class women joined peace societies, the anti-slavery movement, and finally, the women's rights movement. Sarah Grimke traveled the road of consciousness-raising from peace and pacifism to feminism, and was often opposed by males in such movements simply because she was a woman. Lucretia Mott and Elizabeth Cady Stanton had similar experiences before they organized the Seneca Falls Convention in 1848. The convention issued a Declaration of Independence that placed "man" in the role of tyrant, asking most significantly for the "elective franchise." Feminist pressure resulted in several state laws giving women more control over their property and equalizing divorce proceedings. Finally in 1833, women were admitted to full degree programs at Oberlin College. In 1865 Vassar was founded. By that time Antoinette Brown took the first female theology degree at Oberlin, and the two Blackwell sisters were admitted to medical school.

D.   Antislavery Sentiments

An early movement to free slaves that attracted supporters with other motives was the African colonization society which founded Liberia in West Africa. The antislavery movement was linked with perfectionism and converted to a crusade for total abolition. The leader of the crusade William Lloyd Garrison, founder of the Liberator in 1831, the same year that Nat Turner instigated a serious slave uprising in Virginia. Southerners began to view Garrison and his movement with horror; but he persisted, insisting that any constitution which allowed slavery was a "Covenant with Death." Antislavery campaigns were also attacked in the midwest and even New England, which was the center of the movement.

E.   Utopian Socialism

All reform movements attempted to cure some problem in American society without disturbing the structure of the system itself. There were a few who wanted to go further, however, to erase distinctions between rich and poor and to replace competition with cooperation. They lived in utopian communities inspired either by Charles Fourier or the British factory owner Robert Owen. Brook Farm quickly closed its doors, but the Oneida community in New York was an unusual success. Combining evangelism and socialism, the Oneida system reduced work to the essentials; freed from the bonds of marriage, women chose their lovers and husbands. Children were raised in a very open-minded way by the community and schools were allowed great creativity. Shakers organized several religious communities in the 1840s and prospered by selling finely made products. The Amana society in New York, then Iowa, survived until the twentieth century by marketing blankets and woven goods.

VI. **Conclusion:** Americans in the pre-Civil War North and West were competitive, crude, bad-mannered and bigoted; they were also humane, romantic, creative and socially responsible. The main reason for the paradox was the extraordinary change that accompanied rapid urbanization and industrialization in what was still an essentially rural and agricultural society. Native-born Protestants were faced with new immigrants from Europe, many of whom were Roman Catholic. More importantly the North and West were becoming a distinct section that was in many ways quite different from the South.

Learning Objectives

After reading Chapter 12, you should be able to:

1. Contrast Frederick Jackson Turner's theory of frontier individualism with the realities of western life.

2. Describe urban conditions in the Northeast and their effect on migration.

3. Account for the rise of nativism and discrimination against blacks and women.

4. Explain the nature of romanticism, transcendalism and other intellectual trends which influenced the New England Renaissance.

5. List the major authors and artists of the ante-bellum period.

6. Explain both the religious and the secular origins of the reform movement in temperance, asylums, peace and women's rights.

7. Describe the successes and failures of the early antislavery movement.

8. Account for the organization of utopian communities and describe some significant examples.

Identifications

Identify the following terms as you read the chapter; also note the significance of the term.

1.	Harriet Martineau	2.	Alexis de Tocqueville
3.	Frances Trollope	4.	frontier individualism
5.	urbanization	6.	Five Points

7.	Nativism	8.	Jim Crow laws
9.	cult of true womanhood	10.	Washington Irving
11.	James Fenimore Cooper	12.	Edgar Allen Poe
13.	Ralph Waldo Emerson	14.	Nathaniel Hawthorne
15.	Herman Melville	16.	Walt Whitman
17.	Hudson River School	18.	second Great Awakening
19.	Perfectionist	20.	Dorthea Dix
21.	Sarah Grimke	22.	Lucy Stone
23.	William Lloyd Garrison	24.	Frederick Douglas
25.	Seneca Falls Convention	26.	Elizabeth Cady Stanton

Focus Your Reading

Employ the terms you have identified above in answering the following questions:

1. Discuss some of the "democratic" tendencies of Americans noted by observers such as Martineau, de Tocqueville and Turner.

2. Contrast the "democratic" tendencies noted above with the impulses of nativism and Jim Crow policies.

3. Trace the influence of the second Great Awakening on the development of new religious communities such as Oneida, Amana and those developed by the Shakers and the Mormons.

4. How did the second Great Awakening affect the development of social reform efforts such as temperance, asylum/prison reform, and women's rights?

5. Discuss the rise of an American identity in literature, painting and architecture in the 19th century. Who were key representatives in these arts and why?

Questions

---

1. The European writer who remarked that American equality extended to servants who called themselves "help" was
    a. Frances Trollope
    b. Alexis de Tocqueville

c. Harriet Martineau
d. Charles Lyell

2. All of the following constitute reasons that people moved from the East to the West except
   a. a desire to avoid people nearby
   b. restlessness
   c. high land prices in England
   d. escape from legal obligations

3. All of the following were qualities noted in western pioneers by Frederick Jackson Turner except
   a. individualism
   b. dependability
   c. egalitarianism
   d. idealism

4. The main reason that southern plantation owners moved westward was
   a. competition in grain and meat
   b. better sheep pasture
   c. declining soil fertility
   d. pressure from antislavery advocates

5. Immigration to the United States was heaviest in
   a. the pre-Revolutionary War Period
   b. the 1830s
   c. the 1850s
   d. the 1820s

6. The Irish tended to have a harder time making a successful transition to American life before 1860 because
   a. they were Roman Catholic
   b. they were starved out of their homeland and had fewer resources
   c. they never got along with the English
   d. all of the above

7. According to the cult of true womanhood a "true woman"
   a. was one who was free within her sphere
   b. was no longer the object of male domination
   c. was modest, reverent and chaste
   d. used prudery as a defense mechanism

8. Of all the New England intellectuals of the 1840s the only one who refused to pay taxes to support the Mexican War was
   a. Ralph Waldo Emerson
   b. Henry David Thoreau
   c. Nathaniel Hawthorne
   d. George Ripley

9. During the second Great Awakening, the "burnt-over" district of New York produced the new religions known as
   a. Unitarians and Perfectionists
   b. Methodists, Baptists and Presbyterians
   c. Latter Day Saints, Adventists and Shakers

        d.   all of the above

10.   The Seneca Falls convention dedicated to the personal liberation of women was
        organized by
        a.   Lucretia Mott and Elizabeth Cady Stanton
        b.   Angelina and Sarah Grimke
        c.   Frederick Douglass and William Lloyd Garrison
        d.   Antoinette Brown and the Blackwell sisters

11.   The most controversial white abolitionist in the 1830s was
        a.   Horace Mann
        b.   Fredrick Douglas
        c.   William Lloyd Garrison
        d.   Steven Foster

12.   The Shaker Communities believed in all of the following except
        a.   economic cooperation
        b.   spiritual perfection
        c.   abstinence from sex
        d.   complex marriage

Essay

1.   Discuss the main attractions of the West for Americans living in New England, the
        middle states and the South. What was the principal economic factor in westward
        migration? What were secondary factors?

2.   Compare the problems of urban areas in the 1840s with problems in the cities
        today.

3.   Explain discrimination encountered by women in education and professional life in
        the nineteenth century. What efforts were successful in overcoming such
        discrimination? Which was not and why?

4.   Discuss the life of Frederick Douglass. In which ways does he compare to Martin
        Luther King, Jr., and in which ways was he unique?

5.   Trace the development of the anti-slavery movement from the American
        Colonization Society to Garrison's anti-slavery Society and the Liberator. How did
        the abolition movement give rise to the women's rights movement?

CHAPTER 13

The Old South

What Is Myth and What Was Real?

Summary and Outline

Summary: What was the Old South really like? Was it a brilliant society based on mutual respect and high cotton prices, or was it an authoritarian tyranny ruled by a privileged minority who abused their slaves and lorded it over poor whites?

Outline: I. An Unexpected Diversity: The South's warm climate distinguished it from the North and the Midwest; its long growing season made it possible to grow short-fiber cotton and sugar cane. Corn was its chief grain crop and the hog was the basis of its animal husbandry. However, the natural environment was not the main factor that defined the Old South.

A. Southern Agriculture

One myth that persists in modern times is that the Old South was a gigantic cotton field; corn was more important in many ways, however. It fed most of the people and the region's farm animals. Corn was worth $209 million as opposed to cotton, which was valued at $136 million in 1855. But cotton was a cash crop, and as such it was the only farm crop that could enrich those who planted it. Other cash crops such as hemp, sugar, rice and tobacco did not match cotton as a source of income.

B. Industry

Another myth about the Old South was that it was economically backward. Usually historians stressed worn-out cotton lands and the deflection of capital from factories and machines to new land and slaves. Slavery itself was seen as the principal roadblock to investment, industry and incentive-based work. Scholars today see serious flaws in pervious analyses: slaves did much of the same work performed by immigrants and native-born industrial workers in the North. Slaves were paid employees in southern towns and factories; they were miners, deck hands, cotton operatives, and iron workers. Plantations were functioning business organizations managed by practical men; the gap in industrial production between North and South was not a result of aristocratic contempt for commerce and industry but rather the preference of planters for agriculture instead of manufacturing.

C. Social Diversity

Another misconception among scholars concerns the social system of the Old South. The familiar tiers of great planters, slaves and poor whites does not correspond to reality. The aristocracy was very small; the typical slave holder was middle class: seventy-one percent of slave holders had fewer than ten slaves. The non-slave holding yeomanry was even larger, and it was politically influential. However, parts of the old picture remain intact. Wealth was more highly concentrated in the hands of fewer people than in the North.

Small southern farmers were poorer than their northern counterparts; and there was a white lower class. Voting was rigged in favor of the plantation owners in many areas, and small farmers deferred to them. Hinton Helper's Impending Crisis of the South (1857) attacked the planter class on behalf of the yeoman on the eve of the Civil War.

II. **Life Under Slavery:** The old picture of black life under slavery has long been discredited; no one seriously believes that slaves were the beneficiaries of a fundamentally benign system. On the other hand the newer picture of organized terror that subjected black people to constant brutality and degrading labor is not accurate either. Slave life was diverse. Most black people worked in agriculture; but a minority lived in towns, where black leaders were important in urban cultural life. There were 250,000 free blacks in the Old South. A few were successful in business and the professions; and some even owned slaves. Most were unskilled workers who suffered white contempt and had no civil rights. Three-fourths of the South's four million slaves worked on large plantations, mostly as field hands. They were not badly treated on the whole, as they represented a substantial investment for the owner. Slaves who lived in close quarters with their masters were not as well treated as once assumed; small planters were faced with financial problems that often led to the sale of slaves and the breakup of slave families.

A. Slave Culture

Slavery did not prevent the development of an independent, vigorous black culture, which prospered in oral literature and music. Storytellers drew on the West African tradition of "trickster" tales, which they combined with Bible stories. Not only was group identity maintained, but freedom from bondage was made into an underlying theme. Christianity served a similar function; black preachers became social and political leaders. While the masters hoped that blacks would learn submission and obedience from their church attendance, spirituals illustrate how closely slaves identified with the children of Israel in bondage. White masters noted such subversive messages as well and often forebade separate religious services for their slaves.

B. Slavery as a Coercive System

However decent some masters were in regard to housing, food and medical attention, slavery was grounded on coercion. Slaves were punished for stealing, disobeying orders, running away or fighting. Young males were most likely to be singled out for flogging, but no black group was exempt. Rewards rather than punishment were preferred by some planters, who might even allow craftsmen to "hire out," eventually buying their freedom with the proceeds of their skills.

C. Slavery and the Family

Harriet Beecher Stowe's Uncle Tom's Cabin (1852) presented the most memorable image of black family life under slavery when Eliza fled across the frozen Ohio River to save her baby from sale to a brutal white master. Although such things happened, masters usually preferred their slaves to be married, and it seems, so did slaves themselves. White masters sexually exploited black women, but they on occasion took care of them and their offspring. White women deplored miscegenation, and it was seen by both black and white authorities as a disruptive if not scandalous practice.

D. The "Bottom Line" of Slavery

The most recent studies on slavery refute the grimmest assertions of its critics. The slave family survived and prospered. There were opportunities for economic improvement and even free status within the system. Yet it was not a happy system for most people involved in its inner workings. Slavery limited the freedom of blacks to withhold labor, to benefit from it, or to move elsewhere; deprived of "life, liberty and the pursuit of happiness," they could not escape cruelty or torture. They were not taught to read and write, so their abilities were not tested. In the end the worst legacy of slavery was racism, which survived the end of the peculiar institution itself.

III.   The Southern Mind: How accurate is the myth that the Old South was a genial and cultivated society? While there were highly educated people in the Jeffersonian mold, and southerners joined in the reform movements of the 1820s, by 1860 the South had strangled dissent in the name of its principal institution.

A.   Slave Revolts

Most southerners' worst fears were related to slavery. They refused to acknowledge its cruelty, but they all knew that slaves would end the institution if they could. Every day slaves ignored directions, ran away or engaged in slowdowns. Southerners feared slave revolts most of all. In 1800 Gabriel Prossner attempted to capture the city of Richmond. Ten years later 500 slaves started a march against New Orleans and were stopped by troops. In 1822 the planned uprising of Denmark Vesey was foiled by betrayal; thirty-five insurrectionists were hanged. The biggest revolt was planned and executed by Nat Turner in 1831. Sixty Virginia whites lost their lives before Turner and seventy others were captured and executed.

B.   Quieting the Opposition

Soon after Turner's revolt the Virginia legislature debated the possible abolition of slavery. Many western representatives attacked the institution, but to no avail. After 1832 repression began in earnest; slaves were required to carry passes, patrols were increased, and scores of innocent slaves were jailed or executed in panic. All "outside agitators" became suspect, but abolitionists were special targets of Southern legislators. Postal carriers refused to carry antislavery tracts and newspapers. Southern-born critics like James G. Birney, the Grimke sisters and Cassius Clay were driven out. Southerners were even compelled to impose a "gag order" in Congress which prohibited resolutions on slavery from being debated in the House of Representatives.

C.   Arguments in Favor of Slavery.

Southerners had always defended the necessity of slavery in plantation agriculture without actually condoning its morality. After 1800 they began defending it as a Christian institution sanctioned by God in the story of Noah and in the New Testament by Paul's enjoiner to servants to obey their masters . After 1830 a "scientific" argument was devised which was based on the supposed biological inferiority of blacks. George Fitzhugh constructed a sophisticated "sociological" defense of slavery in which it was a "positive good" as opposed to "wage slavery" in the North.

D.   Romance and Culture

Southerners devised literary defenses for slavery from the novels of Sir Walter Scott. They asserted that southern gentlemen were the sons of cavaliers descended from English nobles, while northerners were progeny of Puritan Roundheads. Such notions produced plantations that were feudal manors, planters who were knights and slaves who were serfs. Southern ladies were placed on pedestals and treated with outward gallantry. This social mythology tended to stifle artistic growth in the South; even Stephen Foster was a northerner. Many young southerners went to college in the North to escape the intellectual mediocrity that resulted from the restriction of free inquiry in the south.

E.   Southern Ideology

The South defended its own peculiar institution; but in doing so it was able to detect flaws in the individualistic capitalist system that emerged in the North. Southerners also attacked majority rule partly because they feared losing political equality with the North when one more free state than slave state would be admitted to the Union. Southerners also complained about economic vassalage to northern business interests as northern agents of factors regulated credit and marketing in the cotton trade on a commission basis. De Bow's Review and others proclaimed the need for the South to do its own importing, exporting and banking; they also demanded that the slave trade be reopened. John C. Calhoun in his old age doubted that democracy could work and advocated separated southern voting and a dual presidency, proclaiming that the "best" societies, like Greece and Rome, utilized slave labor to construct admirable civilizations.

IV.   Conclusions: The Old South was neither as idyllic as the advocates of the cavaliers claimed, nor was it as full of brutality as its modern critics contend. It was ruled by a planter elite but with the consent of a large yeoman farmer class. There was a veneer of gracious plantation life; but cotton production was managed by profit-minded owners who viewed their slaves as part of the system. Southern slavery thus avoided the worst abuses of forced-labor industry and agriculture. Southerners knew that black rebellion could erupt at any time, but criticism of the institution of slavery could not be tolerated. It was not long before southerners considered their society one that had little in common with the rest of American and Atlantic culture.

Learning Objectives

After reading Chapter 13, you should be able to:

1.   Separate myth from reality in describing the agriculture, industry and social structure for the South.

2.   Describe the life of black people who were free and those who were slaves.

3.   Explain the survival of an independent black culture and religion

4.   Compare the benign view of slavery with the critical view.

5.   Review the steps by which the South created an intellectual as well as an economic argument in favor of slavery.

6.   Describe the social and political structure of the Old South as it actually existed as opposed to the various theories advanced by previous writers.

Identifications

Identify the following terms as you read the chapter; also note the significance of the term.

1.   drivers
2.   The Impending Crisis of the South
3.   Br'er Rabbit
4.   Uncle Tom's Cabin
5.   miscegenation
6.   Autobiography
7.   Nat Turner
8.   Denmark Vesey
9.   gag rule
10. Shem Ham and Japeth
11. Pro Slavery Argument
12. George Fitshugh
13. James Hammond
14. cavaliers
15. John C. Calhoun

Focus Your Reading

1.   Compare the image of the ante-bellum South with the reality of the plantation system.

2.   What was life like under slavery in terms of family life, religion, culture, and forms of resistance to slavery?

3.   What was the role of Christianity in the organization of a cohesive black community while it was still enslaved? What has been the continuing role of black ministers in modern times?

4.   In which ways was George Fitzhugh correct in his assessment of northern industrialism? In which ways was he incorrect?

Questions

Multiple Choice

1.   Which of the following jobs were performed by slaves?
     a.   drivers or overseers
     b.   coopers or masons
     c.   municipal workers
     d.   all of the above

2. How many large slave holders were there in the Old South?
   a. 2200
   b. 383,000
   c. 200,000
   d. 4 million

3. In order to remove the ruling class from its position in the Old South, Hinton Helper was willing to
   a. give the vote to freed slaves
   b. allow abolitionists free travel in the South
   c. rally non-slave holders against them with the help of slaves
   d. ask the North to send troops to remove them

4. Which of the following now seems correct concerning slave life in the Old South?
   a. it was a system of organized terror
   b. slaves were happy workers who sang while they worked
   c. slave life was diverse
   d. there was mutual respect between master and slave

5. Black culture in the Old South developed all of the following except
   a. songs about daily life
   b. animal tales about the southern environment
   c. poetry about the pleasures of plantation life
   d. songs that expressed the true feelings of the slaves

6. While white masters hoped that Christianity would teach their slaves submission, black Christianity actually
   a. helped to preserve a sense of black independence
   b. produced a message of hope and freedom
   c. produced black leaders among the clergy
   d. all of the above

7. In the long term the system of slavery damaged American society the most because it
   a. separated the country into two political parties
   b. split up black families
   c. reinforced racism
   d. put the South behind the North in industrial development

8. All of the following led southern slave revolts except
   a. John Floyd
   b. Denmark Vesey
   c. Gabriel Prosser
   d. Nat Turner

9. All of the following were used to defend slavery except
   a. the distribution of duties to the sons of Noah
   b. advice in the New Testament for servants to obey their masters
   c. the idea that blacks were closer to "brute creation"
   d. the idea of Perfectionism

10. George Fitzhugh argued that if the North was any example a free society produced
   a. split-up families
   b. slums, social dislocation and wage slavery

c. cooperation rather than competition
d. all of the above

11. The mistress of a southern plantation might expect that her life would be spent
a. working hard in a demanding job
b. at tournaments showering gentlemen with roses
c. asking for help and protection
d. fox hunting

12. John C. Calhoun claimed that the South could save its civilization by
a. increasing democratic rule
b. giving the central government more power
c. requiring that all laws be passed by a "concurrent majority"
d. leaving the union

Essay

1. Discuss at least two controversies in southern history that involve slavery and the plantation system.

2. Explain the argument concerning southern industrialization before 1860. How backward was the southern economy in comparison to the rest of the world.

3. Discuss the life of free blacks in the South. How did their life compare with that of slaves?

4. Discuss the white social structure of the Old South, (planters, small slave holders, yeoman, and people of the pine barrens), their relations with each other and the institution of slavery.

Map Exercises

Locate or draw in the following and explain their significance.

The Old South

1. Missouri

2. Upper South

3. Lower South

4. Tide Water Region

5. Mississippi River

6. Piedmont

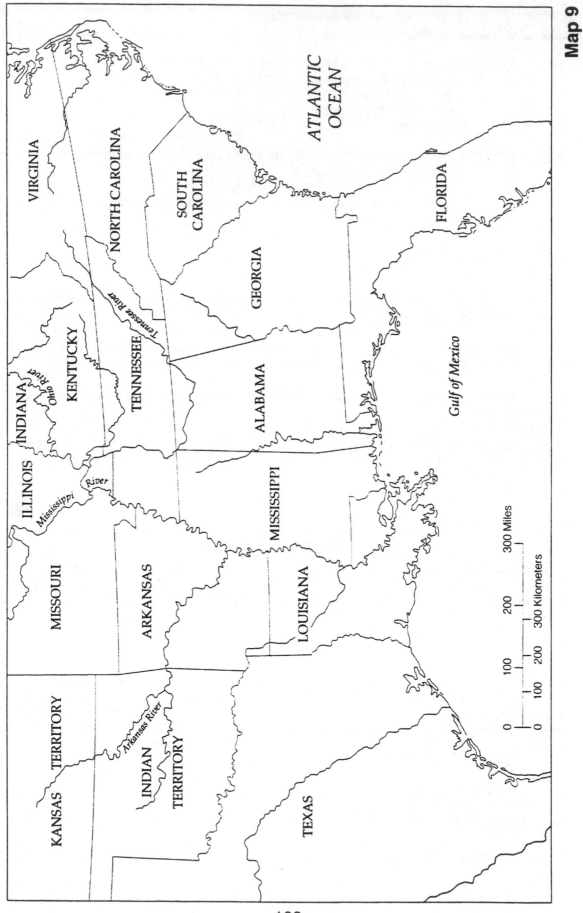

Map 9

VIRGINIA

NORTH CAROLINA

SOUTH CAROLINA

GEORGIA

ATLANTIC OCEAN

FLORIDA

KENTUCKY

TENNESSEE

Tennessee River

ALABAMA

Ohio River

INDIANA

ILLINOIS

Mississippi River

MISSISSIPPI

LOUISIANA

Gulf of Mexico

MISSOURI

ARKANSAS

KANSAS TERRITORY

Arkansas River

INDIAN TERRITORY

TEXAS

300 Miles

0   100   200   300 Kilometers
0   100   200   300 Kilometers

CHAPTER 14

The Coming of the Civil War

What Caused the Division?

Summary and Outline

Summary: When the Civil War started many Americans asked why a nation so self-confident and so triumphant was now involved in a conflict that threatened its very survival. Students of history ask the same question today.

Outline: I. A House Dividing: The sectional conflict that gradually divided North and South in the two decades before 1860, was a product of industrialization and cultural diversity in the former and plantation agriculture and social conformity in the latter.

A.   Ideological Differences

Both sections were culturally and ideologically complex: there were "doughfaces" who supported southern principles in the North and there were small farmers in the South who hared slavery and the planter class. Increasingly, however, majority opinion in the South glorified an agricultural society based on slavery and condemned criticism of such a society. On the other hand in the North a consensus slowly emerged which was based on free movement in a free society, the freedom to speculate, to invest, to take up land, and to advance in one's work.

B.   Economic Conflict

To some extent the gap between North and South was a reflection of economic competition between northern commerce and industry and southern agriculture. The South was able to lower the tariff over the years; but the South fought Northern efforts to import foreign labor and improve rivers and harbors. Southerners also fought a northern transcontinental railroad route and any homestead bill which promised free land in the West.

C.   The Role of Slavery

Clashes over economic policies, tariffs, railroad subsidies or internal improvements are not sufficient to explain why the two sections finally resorted to war. Louisiana sugar planters favored tariffs and Senator Johnson of Tennessee campaigned for the homestead bill. Only in the decade following the Mexican War were grievances converted to outrage in a manner sufficient to bring the South to secede from the Union.

II.   The Dilemma of Territorial Growth: Geographical expansion aggravated the differences between the sections. The Northwest Ordinance of 1787 excluded slavery from the unorganized area north of the Ohio river, while the Southwest Ordinance of 1790 allowed it in the Southwest. The Louisiana Purchase produced one slave state, Louisiana, in 1812, then another, as Missouri was admitted to the Union in 1820. It was agreed in

Congress that the rest of the Louisiana Purchase would be divided along the southern boundary of Missouri (36°30" north latitude).

A.   The Wilmot Proviso

The division between free and slave labor caused no trouble between 1820 and 1835. Then Texas revived the issue when it was admitted to the Union as a slave state, followed by the addition of Oregon, California and New Mexico in the Mexican cession. Congressman David Wilmot of Pennsylvania proposed that slavery be excluded from all such territories in 1846. Southern opposition kept the Proviso from passing in Congress, but the idea of excluding slavery from all Western territories remained a possibility for northerners. In 1847, Lewis Cass of Michigan proposed the concept of popular sovereignty, that is, leaving to the people of any new territory the option of settling the matter of slavery for themselves.

B.   Free Soil

The two political parties tried to avoid the slavery issue in 1848 by nominating heroes or unknowns. The Whigs nominated Zachary Taylor, the hero of Buena Vista, without a platform. The Democrats nominated Lewis Cass, of Michigan, the inventor of popular sovereignty. Martin Van Buren left the Democratic convention and set up a "Barnburner" faction which merged with Free-Soilers from the Whig party. Meanwhile the Liberty Party, organized in 1839 to stop the 'slave power' from dominating Congress, nominated Senator John P. Hale of New Hampshire on an antislavery platform. In a few months the party merged with the Free Soil Party, accepting the ticket of Van Buren and Charles Francis Adams in 1848. Taylor won the election, but the Free-Soilers elected enough members to Congress to provide an outspoken antislavery minority for the decades ahead.

C.   Gold in California

President Taylor, a southern slave holder, was an unexpected strong unionist. In 1848 an employee of John A. Sutter found gold while constructing a waterway near Sacramento, California. A gold rush followed which brought thousands of Americans to the Central Valley, and which prompted Taylor to suggest that California apply directly to Washington for admission to the Union. A constitution excluding slavery was drawn up and sent with an application for statehood to Washington.

D.   Decisive Issues in Congress

Tarlor's scheme to avoid strife in Congress over the admission of California did not work. It set off a fierce controversy. Added to the argument over elimination of the slave trade in Washington D.C., was the South's insistence that fugitive slave laws were not being enforced. Northern "personal liberty laws" were passed to prevent state assistance to federal authorities who attempted to capture runaway slaves. Texas wanted part of eastern New Mexico, which the Free-Soilers opposed. Then there was the question of New Mexico's status: could territories make the decision on slavery for themselves under popular sovereignty?

E.   The Compromise of 1850

Fortunately for the Union, old hands at settling thorny problems were still alive. Henry Clay, the old Whig compromiser, was determined to head off John C. Calhoun's disunionist schemes. To prevent the showdown Clay enlisted the help of fellow Whig statesman Daniel Webster and Democrats Stephen Douglas of Illinois, Thomas Hart Benton of Missouri and Sam Houston of Texas. Free-Soil advocates Salmon Chase of Ohio, Charles Sumner of Massachusetts, and the former Whig governor of New York, William H. Seward, opposed compromise from the free side as strongly as Calhoun opposed it from the pro-slavery side. Clay's Omnibus Bill did not pass at first, but Douglas got each provision passed separately. Meanwhile Millard Fillmore succeeded to the presidency upon the death of President Taylor, and threw his support to Douglas. The Compromise of 1850 admitted California to the Union as a free state, and New Mexico and Utah as territories to decide the status of slavery by popular sovereignty. It awarded Texas $10 million for its creditors, abolished the slave trade in Washington, D.C. and enacted a stiffer fugitive slave law to please the South.

F.   The Fugitive Slave Act of 1850

The Fugitive Slave Act in the Compromise of 1850 inflamed northern resentment against the South as soon as its provisions were known. The law required northern law-enforcement officials to hold suspected fugitive slaves without a trial and cooperate in their capture. When blacks were put in jail in the North to be returned to bondage, many formerly indifferent citizens were converted to antislavery sentiments. Some attacked slave-catchers, hid escapees and took them to Canada. State legislatures passed personal liberty laws which nullified the federal statute. Harriet Beecher Stowe was so shocked by the sight of a returning fugitive slave in Cincinnati that she composed Uncle Tom's Cabin, a tragic story of slavery which sold 300,000 copies in one year. The novel aroused such anger in the North and South that it made the sectional conflict worse. According to legend, Abraham Lincoln acknowledged that Stowe was the "little lady who wrote the big book that caused the war."

III.   Worsening Tensions: The Compromise of 1850, for all its faults, put the slavery issue to rest for several years. However the aged compromisers soon died and Stephen Douglas did not have the skill to save the Union on his own. The Democrat Franklin Pierce was elected President in 1852 as the Whig party fell apart.

A.   Southern Dreams of Empire

Southerners would not leave the issue of slavery extension alone: many supported the purchase of Mexican states or went on filibustering raids into Central America and the Caribbean. In 1854 three pro-slavery diplomats issued the Ostend Manifesto which invited Spain to sell Cuba to the United States. William Walker invaded Nicaragua in 1856 with a private army, hoping to make it a new slave state. Little resulted from these efforts, but they convinced many northerners that slavery advocates would stop at nothing to keep the peculiar institution alive.

B.   The Kansas-Nebraska Act

Senator Stephen Douglas undid his good work on the Compromise of 1850 in 1854 when he introduced a bill to establish a territorial government in the Nebraska Territory based on popular sovereignty. The whole area should have been free soil under the Missouri Compromise; but Douglas was in a hurry to develop the area at any cost to promote quick development of the West and a central route for the transcontinental railroad. Douglas needed southern support for his scheme and repeal of the Missouri Compromise was a condition for this support. Popular sovereignty gave the South a chance to introduce slavery in a previously closed territory. Kansas was not suited to plantation agriculture, but for the South, the issue raised by Douglas became symbolic. Douglas failed to see that northerners would find the issue symbolic as well. President Franklin Pierce put pressure on northern Democrats to endorse the Kansas-Nebraska Act and it passed in May 1854, by a majority.

C.   National Parties Break Up

The Kansas-Nebraska Act strained the bonds of traditional party loyalties beyond endurance; Salmon P. Chase's appeal to independent Democrats labeled the act a criminal betrayal, castigating both Douglas and Pierce. Northern Whigs were even stronger in their antislavery sentiments than the free-soil Democrats. Conscience Whigs clashed with cotton Whigs. As the party broke up, most Whigs joined the new Republican Party which was organized at Ripon, Wisconsin, in 1854. The Know-Nothing Party joined the group along with many northern Democrats.

D.   "Bleeding Kansas"

A few weeks later after the Kansas-Nebraska Act was passed, pro-slavery and anti-slavery groups clashed over conflicting land claims. Two rival governments were set up, one representing a slave state, the other a free state. A civil war ensued punctuated by massacres on both side, the best known of which was the abolitionist John Brown's attack on pro-slavery settlers at Pottawatomie Creek. The Sumner-Brooks Incident: The junior senator from Massachusetts, Charles Sumner, watched the struggle in Kansas with dismay. In a passionate address called "The Crime Against Kansas" he picked out Senator Andrew Butler of South Carolina for special attack, branding him a foolish blunderer and a liar. Preston Brooks, Butler's nephew and a South Carolina congressman, entered the Senate chamber three days after the speech and beat Sumner repeatedly with a cane. New Englanders were outraged and they demanded that something be done to curb the arrogance of the "slave power."

IV.   Republicanism and the Worsening Crisis: Republicans expanded their base as a result of Bleeding Kansas, Uncle Tom's Cabin, and the Sumner-Brooks incident. Radical Republicans were out-and-out abolitionists; others hoped that slavery would die out or at least be prohibited in the territories. In 1856 the Republicans nominated John C. Fremont, who called on Congress to exclude both polygamy and slavery from the territories. James Buchanan was nominated by the Democrats as he was not associated with "Bleeding Kansas." Buchanan took the election; but Fremont carried enough states to fill Southerners with foreboding.

A.   Buchanan's Policies

James Buchanan was perceived as a doughface Democrat, that is, subservient to the South and sympathetic to slavery. Buchanan wanted the question of congressional power over slavery in the territories settled; so at his urging Chief Justice Roger B. Taney and other southern justices concluded in the Dred Scott case that Congress could not prohibit it. Slavery would have to be excluded by state law. Buchanan also accepted the pro-slavery Kansas constitution, only to have it blocked in Congress and eventually rejected by voters.

B.   The Emergence of Lincoln

The Panic of 1857, a natural economic downturn after years of growth, was blamed on the southerners by northern businessmen angry about the lower tariff. Southerners saw the depression as a vindication of the slave economy as they prospered with high world cotton prices. Douglas began losing southern Democratic support when he failed to support the pro-slavery Kansas Constitution. Republicans looked forward to the election of 1860; Seward and Chase seemed to be their front-runners until Abraham Lincoln appeared in

1858 as the Republican Senatorial candidate from Illinois. Douglas and Lincoln debated throughout the state. At Freeport, Illinois, Lincoln asked Douglas what was left of popular sovereignty now that only a state could exclude slavery. He replied that a state need only refuse to enact a slave code to squelch it . This Freeport Doctrine offended southerners but preserved his image among popular sovereignty supporters. Douglas won the Senate seat and the Democratic nomination. However Lincoln became a national figure and the Republican front-runner.

C.   Harper's Ferry

John Brown moved eastward after the Pottawatomie massacre and planned another blow against slavery. He drew up plans to assault the federal arsenal at Harper's Ferry, Virginia, hoping a major slave revolt would follow. He was surrounded by federal troops on October 16, 1859, captured, tried and hanged for treason against the state. Anti-slavery leaders called Brown a hero, but southerners felt their section would no longer be safe in the Union.

D.   The Party Conventions of 1860

The Democratic convention was held in Charleston, South Carolina. Southerners were prepared to leave the meeting rather than see Douglas nominated on a platform of popular sovereignty. The convention broke up and reconvened in Baltimore, where Douglas received the nomination. Southerners held a separate convention and chose John C. Breckinridge of Kentucky as their nominee, running on a platform that called for a federal code protecting slavery in the territories. With the Democratic party split like many other institutions, what would hold the Union together? Some Whigs and Know-Nothings made a valiant attempt to do so: they formed a Constitutional Union party based on unconditional support for the Union. They nominated John Bell of Tennessee and Edward Everett of Massachusetts. At the Republican convention in Chicago, Lincoln's supporters made much of the weaknesses of all other candidates. He was nominated on the third ballot, running quite openly as a northern candidate. His platform, however, was moderate: slavery was to be limited, but no provision was made as to how; disunion was deplored, but the right of state to choose its own institutions was upheld. A homestead law, a high tariff, improvements and a northern railroad route were also endorsed.

E.   The Union Dissolves

No party or candidate advocated secession. Douglas was a unionist, Bell's sole platform was support of the Union, and Lincoln avoided the slavery issue to keep sectional discord to a minimum. Breckinridge was a border candidate, though all secessionists rallied to his support. Lincoln won a clear electoral majority, carrying every free state except New Jersey, which he split with Douglas. Lincoln got 39 percent of the popular vote to Douglas's 29 percent. In every state but Missouri Douglas ran second with only 12 electoral votes. He and Bell won more popular votes for the Union slave states than Breckinridge. Nevertheless, the South went into panic over Lincoln's victory. South Carolina called a secession convention and declared the union "dissolved" as far as it was concerned. The richer slave holders prevailed in similar conventions throughout the region. By February 1, 1861, the lower south claimed to be out of the Union.

F.   Secession Winter

Southerners hovered between hope and apprehension in fear of slave revolts and federal action. The new state officials transferred their loyalties to the states. Southern army officers resigned their commissions and went home. The Confederate States of America were formed in Montgomery, Alabama, in February, in 1861; Jefferson Davis of Mississippi was elected president and Alexander Stephens vice president. A new constitution declared slavery under state protection and forbade bounties, subsidies and protective tariffs. Southern congressmen resigned from the Congress, while in Washington rumors flew that Confederate forces would attack the capital. Buchanan did nothing and blamed Republicans. Unionists worried about the legal and international implications of secession; Lincoln would not back off on the limitations he wanted on slavery and neither side would extend the Missouri Compromise line to the West as suggested in the Crittenden compromise.

G.   Major Anderson's Ordeal

As the crisis deepened all eyes looked toward two federal forts still in Union hands, but located in Confederate territory. In January 1861 Buchanan dispatched an armed merchant steamer to reinforce Fort Sumter in Charleston harbor, South Carolina. It was fired on and turned back, leaving the garrison commanded by Major Robert Anderson in desperate isolation. On March 4, 1861, Lincoln was inaugurated and was very conciliatory in his address. He would not give up any Federal post as that would amount to recognizing Confederate independence, he said. He sent a resupply mission to the fort but reassured state authorities in South Carolina that no arms or troops would be included. Davis believed that Lincoln's request was a ruse and ordered General Beauregard to remove Anderson by force if needed. Anderson turned down the ultimatum and was bombarded for 40 hours. Anderson returned the fire until his ammunition ran out and surrendered on April 13.

V.   **Conclusion:**   The Civil War arrived with the Confederate government's capture of Fort Sumter. It would go on for four years. Why did it happen? Slavery was the most likely answer even if its role was unrecognized as a direct one at the time. The South feared that its economy and society would collapse if slavery disappeared. Northerners feared the "slave powers" on the other hand and the threat of the institutions to free labor and business. Slavery converted the Mexican cession into a constant source of friction between the two sections, and destroyed the prewar political parties. Douglas badly miscalculated the role he might have played as great compromiser; he not only helped to wreck the Union, but his own political career as well.

Learning Objectives

After reading Chapter 14, you should be able to:

1.   List the ideological and economic differences between the North and the South.

2.   Explain the impact of the acquisition of new territories on the slavery issue.

3.   Document the effects of California gold, the slave trade in Washington, D.C. and fugitive slave laws on American politics.

4.   Explain the principal provisions of the Compromise of 1850.

5.   Explain the reasons that Stephen Douglas introduced the Kansas-Nebraska Bill as well as its immediate and long-term impact.

6.   Account for the breakup of the Whig party and the rise of the Republican party.

7.   Discuss the Lincoln-Douglas debates and the role of the Freeport doctrine in Douglas's declining political fortunes.

8.   Explain the party convention process in 1860 and the role of the election in the breakup of the Union.

Identifications

Identify the following terms as you read the chapter; also note the significance of the term.

1.	Wilmot Proviso	2.	Lewis Cass
3.	Liberty Party	4.	Free Soil Party
5.	Compromise of 1850	6.	personal liberty laws
7.	Little Giant	8.	popular sovereignty
9.	Fugitive Slave Act	10.	Uncle Tom's Cabin
11.	Kansas-Nebraska Act	12.	William Walker
13.	Republican Party	14.	Bleeding Kansas
15.	Dred Scott decision	16.	Abraham Lincoln
17.	Lincoln-Douglas Debates	18.	Harper's Ferry

Focus Your Reading

Employ the terms you have identified above in answering the following questions:

1.   What were the ideological and economic differences between the North and the South?

2.   What were the issues addressed by the Compromise of 1850? Discuss each component and its impact on a region.

3.   How did the Kansas-Nebraska Act destroy the fragile sectional harmony of the 1850s?

4.   Imagine you are a college student in Missouri in February of 1861. Write a letter to your parents telling them of your decision to drop out of college and join the army. You may choose either the Union Army or the Army of the Confederacy, but you

must include in your letter the following: a defense or critique of slavery, a discussion of the Missouri Compromise, an analysis of popular sovereignty and its success or failure in Kansas, and the terms of the impact of the Dred Scott case.

5.   Write a short literary answer to <u>Uncle Tom's Cabin</u> from the southern slave owner's point of view. You may want to consider the view point of the southern farmer who owned no slaves.

Questions

Multiple Choice

1.   Which of the following groups in the South despised slavery?
        a.   small black farmers
        b.   large plantation owners
        c.   small planters
        d.   small businessmen

2.   Which of the following created anxiety among southern slave holders?
        a.   European criticisms of human bondage
        b.   abolitionist attacks on slavery
        c.   erosion of slavery in the border state
        d.   all of the above

3.   When did the first territorial crisis over the addition of a new slave state take place?
        a.   Louisiana in 1812
        b.   Missouri in 1820
        c.   Kansas in 1854
        d.   California in 1850

4.   Which congressional resolution proposed to ban slavery in all the territories acquired from Mexico?
        a.   the Wilmot Priviso
        b.   the Tallmadge amendment
        c.   popular sovereignty
        d.   Compromise of 1850

5.   The most controversial portion of the Compromise of 1850 was
        a.   the abolition of slave trading in the nation's capital
        b.   the admission of California to the Union
        c.   the new fugitive slave act
        d.   popular sovereignty in New Mexico

6.   Southern statesmen considered all of the following proposals for the expansion of slavery except
        a.   buying Mexico's two northern provinces
        b.   William Walker's schemes to annex territory in Nicaragua
        c.   inviting Spain to sell Cuba
        d.   occupation of the island of Santo Domingo

7.	Stephen Douglas's most costly miscalculation as a leader interested in preserving the Union was
	a.	the Kansas-Nebraska Bill
	b.	the Compromise of 1858
	c.	his Senate Campaign in 1858
	d.	all of the above

8.	All of the following were involved in "Bleeding Kansas" except
	a.	the New England Emigrant Aid Society
	b.	Beecher's Bibles
	c.	Uncle Tom's Cabin
	d.	the Pottawatomie Massacre

9.	In considering the Dred Scott case the Supreme Court under Chief Justice Taney chose to rule on the constitutionality of
	a.	the Compromise of 1850
	b.	the Missouri Compromise
	c.	the Kansas-Nebraska Act
	d.	popular sovereignty

10.	The Lecompton Constitution which was written as a basis for the admission of Kansas to the Union was
	a.	pro-slavery
	b.	fraudulent
	c.	rejected by Kansas voters
	d.	all of the above

11.	Stephen Douglas inadvertently told Americans how they could keep slavery out of the territories in
	a.	the Kansas-Nebraska Act
	b.	the Wilmot Proviso
	c.	the Freeport Doctrine
	d.	the Ostend Manifesto

12.	A large majority of the American electorate in the 1860 election voted for a candidate who
	a.	wanted to secede from the Union
	b.	wanted to preserve the Union
	c.	wanted to abolish slavery
	d.	wanted to preserve slavery

Essay

1.	Compare the solutions suggested by various political groups for dealing with slavery in the territory acquired from Mexico.

2.	Discuss Stephen Douglas's role in the Kansas-Nebraska Act. What were his political motives in backing a potentially divisive bill? Were the results worth the gamble for Douglas?

3.	Discuss the role of abolitionism in the conflict leading to the Civil War. Was the South correct in any of its assertions regarding anti-slavery people? Use the incident at Harper's Ferry as part of your basis for judgment.

4.   Compare and contrast the following attempts to resolve the issue of slavery: popular sovereignty, Crittendon Compromise, <u>Dred Scott vs. Sanford</u>, and the free soil position. Why did none of them work?

CHAPTER 15

The Civil War

How Did the War Change the Nation?

Summary and Outline

Summary: What was the real impact of the Civil War upon American society and the industrial age that followed it? There was no doubt that the war destroyed slavery, but did it bring any improvement to the life of former slaves? Was it the great watershed between the agricultural and urban-industrial world that many scholars have noted in the past?

Outline: I.   North and South: The Civil War was more than a military conflict; it was a battle fought by two economies, two governments, and two chief executives. Few living in the 1860s believed that the North had any big advantage in the contest; were such contemporary observations accurate or not?

A.   The Balance of Forces

A neutral observer in 1861 would have bet on the South: it a had an abundance of food, animals and cotton to sell England. To win the war it had only to survive; so the South could depend upon inexpensive defensive strategies. The South possessed superior military talent; the "best third" of the officers of the United States Army followed the secession of their home states. Southern common folk were experienced in the use of arms and outdoor living. Northern forces possessed only an economic edge: more population, more factories, more railroads and a higher industrial output. The North would have to bring the war to the South to win.

B.   Leadership

Despite appearances in 1861 the North had an edge: the man who would lead the Union Forces in the trying years ahead, President Abraham Lincoln. He made the right decisions in spite of having to deal with recalcitrant state governors, radicals and conservatives, southern sympathizers and slave emancipation. Lincoln picked his civilian and military subordinates wisely. Seward made an able secretary of state and Chase ultimately made a capable secretary of the treasury. Edwin Stanton was picked to succeed the corrupt Simon Cameron as secretary of war. Ultimately Lincoln also found two capable generals in Ulysses S. Grant and William T. Sherman. Lincoln was at his best interpreting the Union cause as humanity's "last best hope." Jefferson Davis on the other hand damaged the Confederacy's cause more than he helped it.

II.   The War Begins: Lincoln's call for state volunteers to supplement the regulate army was oversubscribed at first. Four more states joined the confederacy, sending thousands of new recruits into the southern army as well. Both Lincoln's and Davis's Congress believed that the war would be short; in such a case short-term volunteers would not need to be replaced. Davis feared it would be otherwise.

A.   Bull Run

Davis was right and Lincoln was wrong. The fighting that followed the first contest at Bull Run was bloody and interminable. At that small creek in Virginia 30,000 Union troops met a smaller confederate force. The green northern volunteers panicked and retreated, provoking a disastrous scene in which civilians found themselves in danger as well. More men were called up by northern governors to put down what seemed to be a rebellion that demanded serious resistance.

B.   Lincoln's Early Commanders

Lincoln's first general, George B. McClellan, pulled the ragtag Union army together by instilling spirit and confidence in his troops. However he was not a skillful field commander. He could barely eke out a standoff in the Peninsular Campaign against generals Robert E. Lee and Thomas "Stonewall" Jackson. General Ulysses S. Grant did somewhat better in Kentucky and Tennessee; but William T. Sherman was pushed back with heavy losses at Shiloh. Lincoln replaced McClellan with John Pope and Henry Halleck, but he could not find a commander to match Lee. When Pope faltered at Second Bull Run, Lincoln recalled McClellan, who proceeded to stop Lee at Antietam, but failed to follow up on the victory. Generals Burnside and Hooker could do no better; the Army of the Potomac was beaten at Chancellorsville.

C.   Union Strategy

When the original strategy of "On to Richmond" failed as a military strategy, the Union administration reviewed its options. General Winfield Scott, the Union commander-in-chief, wanted to squeeze the South slowly to death. Lincoln never adopted the plan, but he used part of it to cut the Confederacy in half along the Mississippi River. In 1863 Grant finally captured Vicksburg, Mississippi and Port Hudson, Louisiana. At sea the Union navy effectively blocked confederate access to guns and manufactured products.

D.   The Naval War

In 1862 a Confederate ironclad ship, the Merrimac, attempted to run the Union blockade at Hampton Roads, Virginia. The Union ironclad Monitor met the Confederate vessel and forced it to withdraw. Union gunboats were able to support Union military operations on the Mississippi; and Union naval vessels participated in amphibious attacks on Gulf and Atlantic ports. The Union blockade was almost complete in 1865, causing many shortages in the Confederacy. The Alabama and other Confederate blockade runners caused extensive damage to northern shipping; but the confederates were never able to challenge the dominance of the Union navy.

E.   The Diplomatic War

Both important European powers supported the Confederacy: it suited British policy and the French were supporting a puppet regime in Mexico. Cotton diplomacy forged a link between southern planters and the British upper classes. However British factories could get cotton from Egypt and India, and wheat, which England also needed, could only be obtained in large quantities from northern farmers in the United States. Moreover the English middle and working classes could not morally support the slave system.. English naval and financial assistance went to the Confederacy until anti-slavery opinion in England and Union military victories shifted British support to the North.

III. **War and Society:** Military and diplomatic battles between the North and South were matched by home front efforts to raise troops, marshal financial resources and manage internal dissent.

A.   Conscription

The war consumed manpower at an alarming rate; both sides used bonuses for enlistment such as money, livestock or bounties. After 1862 conscription became necessary. Confederate draft laws exempted slave overseers, while Union measures allowed paid substitutes. The Civil War was called a "rich man's war and a poor man's fight," even though by social class and occupation soldiers on both sides corresponded closely to other young men in their respective societies. Draft laws aroused resentment in both the North and South; draft riots against blacks and abolitionists erupted in New York City, while in the Confederacy young men avoided military service by hiding in the hills. In both parts of the country conscription was only one of several innovations that increased national over local power.

B.   The Beginnings of Modern National Finance

The public expense of the Civil War was enormous by the standards of previous wars. The Union was paying $2 million per day for munitions at the war's high point. The South could find few borrowers to finance its efforts so the Confederacy printed fiat paper money. After 1863 the South was forced to impress slaves for fortification work and use soldiers for munitions factories. Crops were taken from farmers without payment. The northern treasury under Salmon P. Chase was able to cope with expanded wartime financing much more efficiently than the Confederacy. In 1865 the first internal revenue system was devised and tariff rates were increased. War bonds were issued which raised $2.5 billion. Chase proposed a new banking system to back the Union's need for a stable currency. By June 1863 there were 450 national banks with federal bonds in their reserves, and the federal government returned to the business of regulating the country's banking affairs. Greenback paper money ultimately had to be issued, but the government was able to limit currency depreciation.

C.   The Spreading Rail System

In 1861 the Union had 22,000 miles of railroad track, the world's largest network, but one that was not interconnected. With the South out of the Union a Pacific Railway Act was passed in 1862 that donated 20 million acres of land and $60 million in bonds in private contractors for a transcontinental railroad. Lincoln got congressional authorization to operate existing lines after 1862. His military supervisors built 650 miles of new track which allowed unlimited movement of troops and supplies. In contrast, Davis was unable to coordinate the small southern rail system, causing Confederate troops to do without supplies even when they were plentiful.

D.   Government Becomes Big Business

The Civil War increased the size of the Union government. New agents of the treasury and war departments negotiated thousands of contracts for millions of dollars' worth of items for the military effort. The economy received a shot in the arm that stimulated business growth and standardized and mechanized many production procedures.

121

E.   Organizing Agriculture

While agriculture burgeoned in the North, it declined in the South as transportation systems broke down and slavery eroded with the invasion of northern armies. The departure of men from northern farms while the demand for foodstuffs soared made the widespread adoption of harvesters and movers necessary. With the South out of the Union the government was able to set up an agricultural department and Congress could enact a Homestead Law. The Morrill Land Grant College Act was also enacted, setting aside millions of acres of public land for the support of agriculture and higher education.

F.   The War and Economic Growth

The transformation of the American economy from rural and agricultural to urban and industrial was well underway before 1860. However when the Civil War began, the North's economy surged ahead, while the South's was devastated. The origins of the war may not be found in economic differences, but its outcome tended to favor business and industry over planting and farming.

G.   New Bonds Between Citizens

The war brought northern citizens closer together in a common cause: to assist soldiers in the battlefield with medical care and moral improvement. Voluntary groups also worked to raise civilian morale explaining and defending the Union cause. Intellectuals reversed their criticism of the country's values and attitudes, and young people ended their rebelliousness. The brash Yankee businessman came to be the model for the postwar generation that would build the new commercial-industrial society.

H.   Dissent

Despite patriotic attitudes engendered by wartime cohesiveness, dissent flourished in the North and the South. Ironically repression was stronger in the Union than in the Confederacy. War Democrats followed Stephen Douglas in his support of the Union cause, even after his death in 1861. Peace Democrats, or Copperheads, favored a negotiated truce with the Confederacy with its institutions intact. They fought the National Banking Act, greenbacks and internal revenue bills. Some Copperheads flirted with treason, but most Peace Democrats supported reunification of the Union with Lincoln. Pro-Confederate sentiment was much stronger in the slave states still in the Union. Full-scale guerrilla war broke out in Missouri between pro-Union and pro-Confederate forces. Lincoln employed all the persuasion he could muster to deal with Radicals in his own party and those who favored keeping slavery intact in the border states. Democratic party opposition appeared to be disloyalty to Lincoln and it was difficult for him to resist using military measures against some critics.

I.   Civil Liberties During Crisis

Clement Vallandigham of Ohio was Lincoln's most outspoken opponent. When he demanded a negotiated peace with the Confederacy in 1863, he was promptly arrested by General Ambrose Burnside. When Vallandigham was convicted of disloyalty, Lincoln was embarrassed, but firm in upholding the verdict. He released the Democratic leader and banished him to the Confederacy. Lincoln suspended habeas corpus in areas where pro-Confederacy sympathy was high, and endorsed heavy penalties against those convicted of inducing persons to commit treason.

J.   The Emancipation Proclamation

Lincoln's repressive policies against civil liberties did not outlast the war, but his policies in race relations exercised a profound influence for future generations. Lincoln tread softly as long as the border states were still considering secession, even overruling Fremont's emancipation of Missouri Slaves in 1861. However as Union troops advanced, slaves flocked to the Union lines, depriving the South of its principal labor supply. Moreover liberated blacks could replace men lost on the battlefield in the North. Emancipation would turn the war into a war for human freedom, making it more difficult for Europeans to support the South. Lincoln decided to use the defeat of Lee at Antietam in 1862 to declare all slaves in every part of the South in rebellion to be"thenceforward and forever free."

K.   The Home Fronts

Virtually every southerner suffered hardships as a result of the war. Southern living standards declined as the blockade took effect and its transport system broke down. In the North prosperity was evident everywhere in 1863; there was an oil boom in Pennsylvania and farm prices were so high that new prairie lands were opened. Employment boomed, especially for women in the medical and nursing fields. Southern women were not employed officially in the war effort, but they were enthusiastic supporters of the Confederate cause.

IV.   The Last Years of Battle: Lee's defeat of Hooker at Chancellorsville raised the spirits of the Confederacy; but the southern government felt that a bold move was necessary to relieve pressure from Grant's forces in the West, to encourage peace-minded groups in the North and perhaps to capture Philadelphia or Washington. Lee's plan to invade southern Pennsylvania was adopted. When Lee moved his forces into position, Lincoln replaced Hooker with Major General George Meade.

A.   Gettysburg

Meade was a competent commander. He deployed his forces at Gettysburg across Lee's line of advance. Meade had new rifles and superior artillery, which sent each Confederate charge back with fearful losses. The last valiant southern effort to unseat the Union was Pickett's charge, which cost the Confederates thousands of lives. Lee retreated just as Grant's forces captured Vicksburg. In the fall of 1863 Grant and General Thomas pushed the Confederate forces out of Tennessee. In March 1864 Grant became commander of all Union forces.

B.   "Johnny Reb" and "Billy Yank"

Gettysburg was the turning point of the Civil War. Johnny Reb and Billy Yank would have several months of fighting left; Billy Yank had the better time of it, but life in the Union forces was not a picnic. Johnny Reb was much worse off, lacking shoes, clothing, food, even ammunition. Veterans did not recall their days in the war with great fondness.

C.   Black Soldiers

Southerners lacked two groups in the Confederate army that brought diversity and strength to the Union army: blacks and foreigners. The Union's greatest manpower reserve consisted of free blacks and former slaves. Denied front-line duty at first and then paid as second-class troops, they nonetheless established a record of "important if not indispensable" service to the Union cause, as Lincoln noted. The valor of black and foreign-born troops had a favorable impact on ethnic and racial attitudes in the North following the war.

D.   The Election of 1864

The election was held as usual in the waning days of the war. Lincoln was renominated with Andrew Jackson, A Unionist from Tennessee, as his running mate. He was opposed by War Democrat George B. McClellan and George Pendleton of Ohio, who favored a negotiated peace with the Confederacy. Two months before the election, General Sherman captured Atlanta, cutting the Confederacy in two. Republican morale was lifted and Lincoln won a popular majority of 400,000 votes.

E.   Last Battles, the Last Casualty

Southern hopes collapsed two months after Lincoln's re-election. General Sherman left Atlanta in flames and marched to the sea, living off the Georgia countryside and destroying southern morale by massive destruction of property. Grant joined Sherman in Georgia after Savannah was captured: General Thomas defeated Hood's army at Nashville. Grant subsequently confronted Lee in Virginia and defeated his army at Five Forks. On April 2, 1865, Confederate officials began abandoning Richmond. On April 7 Lee asked Grant for terms; the two generals met at McLean's in the hamlet of Appomattox Court House, where Grant accepted the surrender of Lee's forces. Lincoln visited Richmond a few days later and made a speech on the subject of reconstruction. On April 14, 1865, he went to the theater with his wife Mary to see the British comedy Our American Cousin. During the third act he was felled by a single shot and died the next morning. John Wilkes Booth, and actor and Confederate sympathizer, had concocted a plot to kill Lincoln, Johnson and secretary of state Seward. All the other officials survived; Booth himself died by his own hand or was killed by a grieving Union soldier.

V.   Conclusions: The threat of permanent national dismemberment was ended. The Civil War fused the nation into a more solid social and economic whole; it helped to create a national banking system, a new currency, a transcontinental railroad, and a new society committed to the values of industrial expansion. Most importantly, the war destroyed slavery, replacing rigidly prescribed racial relations with a system that was at least subject to reform and improvement.

Learning Objectives

After reading Chapter 15, you should be able to:

1.   Compare the advantages of the South with the North at the outbreak of war.

2.   Describe the problems that each side had raising armies.

3.   Trace Lincoln's experiences with his generals from Winfield Scott to Ulysses S. Grant.

4.   Explain the North's strategy in the war and the South's responses to it.

5. Analyze the financial and organizational changes which occurred in Washington as a result of the war.

6. Describe the diplomatic relationships of the North and the South.

7. Explain the need for slave emancipation and its impact.

8. Compare the leadership of Abraham Lincoln and Jefferson Davis.

Identifications

Identify the following terms as you read the chapter; also note the significance of the term.

1.	brother's war	2.	Robert E. Lee
3.	Jefferson Davis	4.	Abraham Lincoln
5.	Ulysses S. Grant	6.	George B. McClellan
7.	Thomas J. (Stonewall) Jackson	8.	Merrimac and Monitor
9.	Charles Francis Adams	10.	New York Draft Riots
11.	greenbacks	12.	Pacific Railway Act
13.	Homestead Act	14.	Emancipation Proclamation
15.	Antietam	16.	Dr. Elizabeth Blackwell
17.	Clara Barton	18.	George Meade
19.	Gettysburg	20.	Vicksburg
21.	Thirteenth Amendment		

Focus Your Reading

Employ the terms you have identified above in answering the following questions:

1. Discuss the military advantages and disadvantages of each side at the start of the Civil War.

2. What was the primary issue of the war and how was that issue supplanted in the middle of the war?

3.	Discuss the military strategies utilized by both sides. Should Lee have struck the North earlier instead of using defensive strategies?

4.	Was the Civil War the last of the old stand-up wars which included gentlemen's agreements and chivalrous attitudes, or was it the first of the modern wars in which no quarter was given to the enemy in pursuit of complete victory? Give example for your position either way.

Questions

Multiple Choice

1.	In a wartime situation the Confederate states had all of the following advantages except
	a.	an abundance of food
	b.	cotton to sell to Europeans for hard cash
	c.	extensive railroad mileage
	d.	interior lines of communication

2.	Jefferson Davis's wartime leadership was qualified by
	a.	his tendency to have his hand in everything
	b.	his less than statesmanlike appearance
	c.	his lack of military experience
	d.	his scant political background

3.	The response to Lincoln's firm resolve to put down the rebellion of southern states was
	a.	over subscription of northern militia quotas
	b.	the secession of four more states
	c.	the rush of southerners into the Confederate army
	d.	all of the above

4.	The man that Lincoln picked to be his first commander of the Army of the Potomac was
	a.	Winfield Scott
	b.	Irvin McDowell
	c.	George B. McClellan
	d.	Robert E. Lee

5.	The First successful strategy that was used by the North against the South was
	a.	the march directly towards Richmond, Virginia
	b.	the two battles fought at Bull Run
	c.	the offensive to cut the Confederacy in half on the Mississippi
	d.	the western attack at Shiloh Church, Tennessee

6.	The British would have continued to support the Confederacy with arms and money were it not for
	a.	the persuasive skills of Charles Francis Adams
	b.	the anti-slavery movement in England
	c.	Union victories in the battlefield

        d.   all of the above

7.   Which statement is the most correct concerning government action during the Civil
        War?
        a.   the Union violated the civil rights of many citizens
        b.   the Confederacy bypassed private enterprise and property rights
        c.   neither side took any action that might be considered excessive
        d.   both sides violated civil rights and property rights

8.   The main impact of the railway system on the war was
        a.   the rapid movement of troops and supplies in the North
        b.   the efficient maintenance carried out by the Confederacy
        c.   to allow families on both sides to visit soldiers
        d.   the replacement of water transportation in the south

9.   With the South out of the Union the northern Congress was able to pass
        a.   a high protective tariff
        b.   a homestead law for western land
        c.   laws for internal improvement
        d.   all of the above

10.   Lincoln considered the Emancipation Proclamation "absolutely essential for the
        salvation of the Union" in 1863 because
        a.   he hoped that the end of slavery would shorten the war
        b.   once blacks realized they were free they would stop working for the
                Confederacy
        c.   it would turn the war into a crusade for humanity
        d.   all of the above

11.   Who supervised the 10,000 nurses and others who assisted the Union wounded
        during the Civil War?
        a.   Clara Barton
        b.   Elizabeth Blackwell
        c.   Dorthea Dix
        d.   Mary Boykin Chestnut

12.   Who does the author of the text regard as the "last casualty" of the Civil War?
        a.   Jefferson Davis
        b.   Abraham Lincoln
        c.   Robert E. Lee
        d.   Ulysses S. Grant

13.   Black soldiers during the Civil War
        a.   served in segregated units
        b.   were paid less than white soldiers
        c.   served often with distinction
        d.   all of the above

Essay

1.   Describe the course of the Civil War by breaking up your analysis into two parts:
        from Fort Sumter to Gettysburg, and from Gettysburg to Appomattox Court
        House. What was different about the two parts?

2. Compare and contrast the leadership of Jefferson Davis and Abraham Lincoln. Which man had the best resources in terms of manpower and industry? Who utilized them better? Which man handled dissent and criticism better? Use examples to back up your opinions.

3. How did the North finance the war? How did the South finance the war? Which system worked better and why?

4. What was the most important effect of the Civil War: the end of slavery, the expansion of government, the end of national disunity or the boost it gave to the new commercial and industrial society of the north? Back up your view with observations of contemporary society.

Map Exercises

Locate the following.

<u>The Civil War</u>

1. Ohio River

2. States that seceded before April 1861

3. States that seceded after April 1861

4. Montgomery

5. Richmond

6. Washington

7. Gettysburg

8. Vicksburg

9. Atlanta

10. Missouri, Kentucky, Maryland, Delaware (Border States)

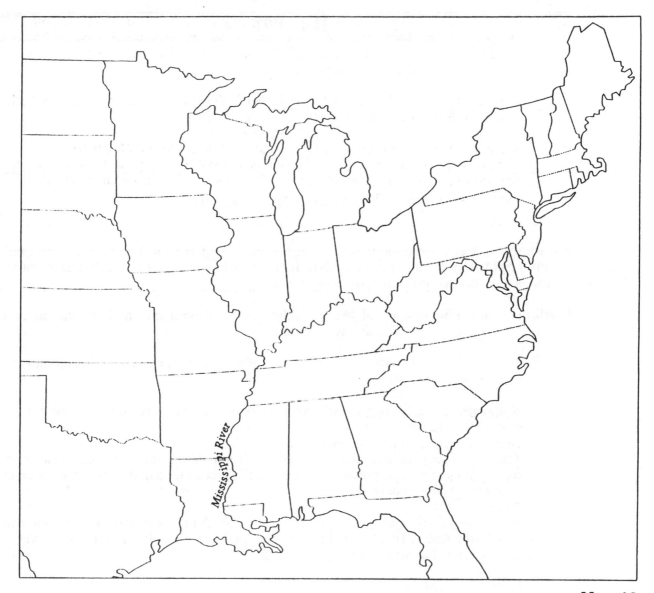

Mississippi River

Map 10

CHAPTER 16

Reconstruction

What Went Wrong?

Summary and Outline

Summary: Reconstruction was not a highly regarded period in American history until the civil rights movement of the Kennedy-Johnson era. What was so unfortunate about the period, and was it as bad as its critics say it was?

Outline: I. The Legacy of War: The South suffered ruin and desolation as a result of the northern invasion during the war.

A.   The end of slavery meant the destruction of the southern labor system and most of its   economic support structure.

B.   Both sides in the Civil War harbored resentments which were central to the political struggles of the Reconstruction era.

C.   The American people faced the task of physical, political and emotional restoration for twelve years. The problems faced and decisions made in the Reconstruction era continue to cause controversy today.

II.   Issues and Attitudes: The main issues most Americans had to deal with after 1865 involved the role of free blacks in the restored Union. Five different points of view reflected the sectional attitudes of Reconstruction.

A.   Radical Republicans

Northerners who blamed the leaders of the Confederacy for the consequences of the war wanted to make sure that free blacks were assisted by the government to full freedom and protected against exploitation.

B.   Northern Conservatives

Former northern Democrats wanted to get the South back into the Union on its own terms; they regarded the rights of former slaves as secondary

C.   Southern Conservatives

Former Confederate activists believed that the South should return to as much of it prewar political and economic structure as possible with no voting rights or economic equality for former slaves.

D.   Southern Unionists

Southerners who opposed secession believed that they should be rewarded for their loyalty; they believed that black people should be given political rights under their leadership.

E.   Southern Freedmen

Former slaves believed that they should be guaranteed equal political and economic rights and protected by the federal government from resurgent power of southern Conservatives.

III.   Presidential Reconstruction: Before his death, Lincoln planned to readmit the southern states into the Union with as little military as practicable.

A.   Lincoln's Ten Percent Plan

Lincoln allowed several states back in the Union when a number of citizens equal to ten percent of those who voted in 1861 took an oath to support the Constitution and establish a new state government free of slavery. Lincoln's plan based on his belief that the southern states were never legally out of the Union, suited his forgiving and practical nature. However the Radicals in his party insisted that the southern states be treated like "conquered provinces" in which citizens would have to swear oaths of past loyalty and recognize the civil rights of freedmen to be admitted to the Union.

B.   Johnson's Plan

Johnson was no Lincoln (as President Ford would later lament); he was anti-black, pro-states rights and susceptible to flattery by aristocratic southerners. In May, 1865, he pardoned most southern leaders and proposed a Reconstruction Plan that could bring southern states back into the Union on a lenient basis, including state conventions, loyalty oaths and the vote for educated blacks.

C.   The Johnson Governments

The new southern governments offended many northerners when they elected several former Confederate leaders to national and state office, then passed Black Codes which restricted the legal and economic rights of former slaves. It must be recalled that a majority of white voters in the northern states also opposed granting full voting rights to black citizens.

IV.   Congress Takes Over: When they returned to Washington in December, 1865, Radical and Moderate Republicans were alarmed by President Johnson's evident sympathy for former Confederates and refused to seat the southern Congressional delegation. The first act of the Congressional Joint Committee on Reconstruction was to extend the life of the Freedman's Bureau and bestow full citizenship on former slaves.

A.   The Fourteenth Amendment.

The Radicals redefined citizenship in a new constitutional amendment which excluded former rebels from office and limited the power of states to deprive any person of life, liberty or property without due process of law.

B.   The First Reconstruction Act

Despite considerable efforts on behalf of President Johnson by the reconciliation-minded National Union Executive Committee and Johnson's own vigorous campaign, the Radical Republicans won a decisive majority in the 1866 Congressional elections. Congress voided the Johnson governments in its March, 1867, Reconstruction Act, which was passed over Presidents Johnson's veto. It divided the South into five military districts with power given to generals to enforce voting rights for blacks and readmit southern states to the Union only when constitutional conventions met and ratified the fourteenth amendment.

C.   Johnson Impeached

When President Johnson took steps to temper the Congressional Plan of Reconstruction, Congress responded with an attempt to convict the President of "high crimes and misdemeanors" for removing Secretary of War Stanton, thus violating the Tenure of Office Act . Although impeached, President Johnson was not convicted.

V .   Reconstruction in the South: When President Grant took office in 1869, the South was reconstructed in a legal sense, but few basic problems had been addressed.

A.   Economic Recovery

Though it remained largely agricultural, the South recovered its economic prosperity by the 1880s.

B.   Tenantry and Sharecropping

The Northern Republicans tried to encourage the growth of a Black Yeoman class, but few freedmen could accumulate enough money to buy land. Many became tenants who paid rent, or sharecroppers, who turned over their crops to the landowner for about half the proceeds. The system had disadvantages for blacks and whites alike, and is generally conceded to be the main reason for the low state of the southern economy for many years following Reconstruction.

C.   Cultural Change

Though segregated from whites, blacks made significant gains as a result of the end of slavery: some left the South to search for jobs elsewhere, others built new black churches, and about half learned to read and write by 1900.

D.   Southern Radical Governments

Blacks never dominated Reconstruction governments as one myth held for many years. Neither were the black legislators who served in those years usually corrupt to incompetent. "Scalawags" were actually prewar Whig business leaders who supported pro-business Republican policies, while "Carpetbaggers," denounced by southern conservatives as "vagrant interlopers," were often sincere northerners who hoped to create a new social order in the South. In general, the Radical-dominated governments were effective, reasonably honest, and more democratic than the ones that preceded them.

E.   "Redemption"

Southern Conservatives moved to "redeem" the southern states from blacks and northern Republicans in the late 1860s. At first, they used hoods and night rides to intimidate black voters; then they ostracized fellow whites who supported blacks and Republicans. Most states were "redeemed" in this manner by 1876.

F.   The End of Reconstruction

Grant-era corruption joined fatigue and racism to bring about the end of Reconstruction. No small consideration was the commercial and industrial development that would follow a formal end to federal control of the South known as the Compromise of 1877.

VI.   Conclusions: Reconstruction produced the three great amendments that continue to provoke civil rights debates today. It gave black people, especially women, their first taste of freedom and political responsibility. However, Reconstruction also produced a legacy of sectional hatred that held back blacks and whites until modern times.

Learning Objectives

After reading Chapter 16, you should be able to:

1.   List the five political groups that interacted within the sectional politics of the Reconstruction Period.

2.   Define Presidential Restruction as it was conceived by President Lincoln and enacted by Andrew Johnson.

3.   Define Congressional Reconstruction as it was conceived by the Radical Republicans and put into force under military rule.

4.   Describe the conditions of Southern Reconstruction and its consequences on both black and white participants.

5.   Analyze the reaction of white southerners to Reconstruction and the political legacy resulting from that reaction.

6.   Identify the effects of Reconstruction policies and institutions upon the black citizens of this country to the present day.

Identifications

Identify the following terms as you read the chapter; also note the significance of the term.

1.   freedmen   2.   carpetbaggers

3.   Wade-Davis Bill   4.   Andrew Johnson

5.   Black Codes   6.   Freedman's Bureau

7.	Thirteenth Amendment	8.	Civil Right Act, 1866
9.	Fifteenth Amendment	10.	Tenure of Office Act
11.	Edwin Stanton	12.	impeachment
13.	Ulysses S. Grant	14.	Share-crop lien
15.	exodusters	16.	Civil Rights Act (1875)
17.	Blanche K. Bruce	18.	Ku Klux Klan
19.	Compromise of 1877	20.	"second Restruction"
21.	"Grantism"		

Focus Your Reading

Employ the terms you have identified above in answering the following questions:

1. Compare the Reconstruction Plans of Lincoln and Johnson with the more punitive plan of Congress.

2. Discuss the success and failure of Reconstruction for the newly freed slaves and for the Democratic party.

3. Trace the development of the impeachment of Andrew Johnson. Explain how a states rights southerner came to be President during this time?

4. Discuss the process of impeachment as it relates to the struggle between Congress and the Presidency. Why was Andrew Johnson impeached?

Questions

Multiple Choice

1. What did most historians believe about reconstruction in the first half of the twentieth century?
   a. Reconstruction nullified the advantages of black emancipation
   b. Reconstruction subjected the South to cruel Northern Occupation
   c. Republican state office holders in the South were moved by revenge
   d. Republicans missed a chance to modernize the South

2. According to Lincoln's plan of 1863, how would a southern state go about restoring itself to the Union?

a. a majority of white males who supported the federal Constitution could call a state convention, but Confederate office holders would be excluded
b. any group of former voters in a Southern state could set up a new state government as long as it excluded slavery
c. Lincoln had to approve all applications to join the Union
d. ten percent of those who voted in 1860 had to take an oath to support the federal Constitution and accept the end of slavery

3. What was the Johnson plan for allowing southern states back into the Union?
a. the president had to approve all applications to rejoin the Union; only the thirteenth amendment need be approved
b. a provisional governor would call a state convention whose delegates would be chosen on the basis of a loyalty oath
c. state conventions would be called by a majority who supported the federal Constitution but were never officers or soldiers in the Confederacy
d. only white males who were not Confederate officers and would support black voting rights could set up new Southern governments

4. Which of the following incidents offended northern Republicans when new southern state governments were set up under Johnson's plan?
a. former Confederate officers were elected to state offices
b. Confederate Congressmen were elected to the U.S. Congress
c. Black Codes placed freedmen in a position of legal inferiority
d. all of the above

5. The main function of the Freedman's Bureau was:
a. to punish southerners who discriminated against freedmen
b. to provide refugee aid, employment and transportation for displaced southerners, black and white
c. to interpret Reconstruction policy for the state governments
d. all of the above

6. Why was the Fourteenth Amendment necessary when the Thirteenth Amendment abolished slavery in 1865?
a. the federal courts were not sympathetic to Republican parties
b. the Thirteenth Amendment did not guarantee equality to freedmen
c. the federal government did not have the power to keep states from depriving persons of life. liberty or property without due process of law
d. all of the above

7. What does the Constitution provide in cases of impeachment?
a. all civil officers can be removed from office on impeachment for, and conviction of, treason, bribery, or other "high crimes and misdemeanors"
b. only the President can be impeached; his cabinet officers must be tried by Grand Juries or Special Prosecutors
c. presidents can only be removed from office if proved guilty of "murder, mayhem or fraudulent behavior" in time of crisis
d. impeachment is not actually provided for in the Constitution

8. The attitude taken by Republican radicals concerning Andrew Johnson's impeachment trial was:
a. conviction would set a bad precedent
b. acquittal would be a victory for rebels and traitors
c. Stanton clearly violated the Tenure of Office Act

d.   all of the above

9.   Why did no large black yeoman class appear?
      a.   lands open to black homesteading were infertile and isolated
      b.   Republicans were too committed to property rights to take land from large
            farmers and give to small farmers
      c.   the bank set up to loan money to freedmen collapsed in the Panic of 1873
      d.   all of the above

10.   "Redeemers" used all but which of the following methods to return control of state
      governments to white southerners:
      a.   hooded riders who attacked black and white leaders
      b.   leaflets asking voters to abandon the Republican Party
      c.   social ostracism of whites who supported northern leaders
      d.   intimidation of black workers who voted

11.   The political tactic known as "waving the bloody shirt" was:
      a.   an appeal to northern voters to reject southern Democrats
      b.   a reminder that southern Democrats were responsible for the war that took
            northern lives
      c.   a ploy to take voters' minds off the scandals of the Grant administration
      d.   all of the above

12.   What was the principal reason that the Compromise of 1877 ended Reconstruction
      in the South?
      a.   Hayes was a better man than Tilden
      b.   southern Whigs wanted a new railroad
      c.   fatigue and racism weakened the resolve of Northern Republicans
      d.   black citizens had achieved the goal of equality

Essay

1.   Review in detail the provisions of the post-Civil War Constitutional Amendments.
      Which had the biggest impact on the political and social system of the United States
      in later years?

2.   Compare the benefits of Radical Reconstruction with its drawbacks. Consider both
      black and white populations in the South.

3.   Discuss the use of the Ku Klux Klan to promote the Democratic Parties agenda of
      white supremacy and the process of "redemption."

4.   Which group had the best reason to be disappointed by the unfulfilled promise of
      the Reconstruction period, blacks or women? Explain how crushed expectations
      played a role in each case.